THE
CUSTOMER
PREVENTION
CULTURE

STOP SABOTAGING YOUR BUSINESS
AND CONQUER COMMERCE

TOM HALPIN

Printed and bound in Canada
Published by Momentum Books, L.L.C., a subsidiary of Hour Media, L.L.C.
5750 New King Drive, Suite 100
Troy, MI 48098

ISBN-978-1-938018-14-5
LCCN: 2019905500

TABLE OF **CONTENTS**

DEDICATION

I'm dedicating this book to my wife, Heather, the most supportive woman on the planet. In addition to her unwavering confidence in me, her ideas and suggestions to expand the concepts in the book were huge and I wouldn't have gotten there without her.

ACKNOWLEDGMENTS

Special thanks to Jason Gingery, Brian Black and Ryan Gingery for their willingness to read the manuscript and provide feedback. Thanks to recording engineer Tommy Halpin for helping me with the audiobook. Props to Don Duncan for sharing his wisdom so many years ago! Heaps of praise to Dave Martzolff, my longtime creative partner, for using his gifts to bring my concepts to life.

Finally, I want to thank my family, friends and colleagues for their encouragement along the way. They listened to my ideas, reacted to them and, by doing so, made them better.

I am blessed to have all of you in my life.

WHO SHOULD READ *THE CUSTOMER PREVENTION CULTURE*SM?

I wrote this book for the humble leaders unafraid to be refreshingly honest about what's broken in their business. For those of us who have overcome significant challenges, we know it starts with an admission of reality. I've been there myself and know humility is more of an asset than a liability. It's impractical and too heavy a burden to think we can have all the answers. Therefore, we need to look outside of our organization to benchmark best practices, seek out thought leaders and join networking forums to share information and discover how peers are dealing with similar challenges to advance their business. We need to become lifelong learners, understand failure is part of the learning process and take calculated risks to avoid complacency. Frankly, this mindset is not only effective in business, but also in life. My hope is The Culture of CommerceSM becomes the standard for driving customer experience through elevated and aligned team performance.

My goal is for B2B manufacturers, distributors and service providers to benefit from *The Customer Prevention Culture*SM in a significant way. Although readers will be exposed to the occasional business-to-consumer (B2C) example, they exist for a quick connection to the book's principles and are easily transferable to B2B environments.

Certainly, leadership teams will learn a lot from the book, especially sales, marketing and customer service leaders. Owners, presidents, operations and human resource leaders struggling with organizational alignment will also gain valuable insights. As an example, one idea highlighted by *The Customer Prevention Culture*SM is that we're all in sales because our workflows are interdependent and ultimately affect the customer experience. Expanding on that point, we ALL have a customer, whether internal or external, which means our workflows interconnect in the value stream and we need to embrace that truth. Otherwise, we're operating in tribes and silos rather than as one team with one goal working toward a shared organizational outcome. But that only addresses the misalignment of people. Add process and technology to the mix, and I'd suggest that all misaligned resources make up the largest productivity drain in the history of mankind with losses that are incalculable. Why? Because misalignment creates friction in the customer experience and slows down commerce. But there is hope! The remedy is The Culture of CommerceSM, which provides a standard for organizations to aspire to and align around to build culture, drive sales and create disciples. As The Culture of CommerceSM transforms the atmosphere in which companies sell, deliver and interface with customers, The Sales EngineSM is able to fire on all cylinders.

Companies struggling with the following scenarios will walk away with answers from reading *The Customer Prevention Culture*[SM]:

- Inconsistent sales results
- Dysfunctional company culture
- Delivering an inconsistent and sometimes painful customer experience
- Misaligned people, process and technology, causing resources to be at odds with one another
- Sales teams spending more time selling internally than externally
- Businesses with innovative commercial offers, but lacking sales and marketing know-how
- Those late to adapt their sales and marketing models to the digital buyer
- Deploying a circa 1985 sales model and questioning why sales results are weak
- Lacking a cohesive sales and marketing framework with measurable ROI
- Inability to scale because of the high cost of selling through a single sales channel
- An openness to change, but lack frameworks to follow

The core of this book is about customer acquisition, customer retention and the dynamics teams must fight through to accomplish both successfully. In the end, the customer must be king, and a company's people, process and technology must serve the customer. As soon as organizations lose sight of this essential truth, troubles surface, and when allowed to persist, they spread throughout the enterprise. The Customer Prevention Culture[SM] is made up of dysfunctional norms that become accepted over time and create friction throughout the customer experience. This book provides a framework to deliver a frictionless customer experience by continually shedding light on The Customer Prevention Culture[SM] and redirecting teams to a higher standard that shapes an organizational way of life.

INTRODUCTION

Throughout my career, I've been amazed at the amount of time and energy sales teams expend insulating customers from internal friction. Rather than selling externally, salespeople spend excessive amounts of effort internally overcoming misalignment and cultural blind spots. In the process of teaching clients how to facilitate commerce, it's become evident that B2B companies everywhere get in their own way at great expense. This is what I call The Customer Prevention Culture^{SM}, and it's embodied by passive leadership, fixed mindsets and delivering a friction-filled customer experience.

The Customer Prevention Culture^{SM} is rooted in the following dysfunctional patterns:

- The Customer Is NOT King! – A desensitization to the fact that the customer is the reason for the company's existence.
- Company-Centric Infrastructure – The company's people, process and technology serve the company's internal stakeholders rather than the customer.
- Tribes & Silos – Misalignment of people and a lack of shared organizational outcomes among team members.
- Customer Touchpoints Break Confidence – The existence of friction throughout too many customer touchpoints, causing the erosion of customer confidence.
- No Values to Form Culture – There is no vision for culture and no proactive pursuit of values to form culture. This gap makes it impossible to inspire team members to a higher cultural standard.

Unfortunately, The Customer Prevention Culture^{SM} is more the norm than the exception in the B2B marketplace. However, for leaders unwilling to accept mediocrity, I offer a solution called The Culture of Commerce^{SM}.

The Culture of Commerce^{SM} is focused on every interaction in the customer experience, whether physical, digital, verbal or written. This mindset attempts to grease the skids of commerce by increasing flow and decreasing friction within the organization.

Culture is a funny thing. It's not tangible, but it certainly can be experienced. And here's the deal: The reality is that culture must be taught, monitored and reinforced by leaders with regular training supported by clearly stated values and outcomes in mind. It needs to permeate all decisions within the business. Otherwise, people are left to their own devices with no collective standard to guide their behavior, attitudes and decision-making. Trust me, if you expect people to use common sense or rise to the occasion, prepare to be disappointed.

Quite frankly, this is how most companies choose to exist. They're so laser-focused on the big picture, managing to metrics or reacting to the issues of the day, that culture gets lost in the process. The Culture of Commerce^{SM} directs the intelligent allocation of enterprise resources to create alignment companywide. It's a guiding philosophy that shapes people, process and technology so trust and credibility are built into the customer experience. The Culture of Commerce[SM] is an atmosphere that enables commerce through the best possible customer experience at all touchpoints of the customer life cycle. Selling, like relationships, is not one and done. It's forever. The Culture of Commerce[SM] helps leaders think through their own culture to identify gaps between reality and their vision for customer experience.

It would be incomplete to discuss The Culture of Commerce[SM] without also sharing a mechanism to create predictable sales results. In this book, we complete the circuit by introducing The Sales Engine[SM], the roadmap to sales predictability, which is an irrefutable sales framework for B2B companies engaged in solution-based, consultative and transactional selling scenarios. The Culture of Commerce[SM] lubricates The Sales Engine[SM] to maximize the flow of commerce. The Sales Engine[SM] is a sales model and The Culture of Commerce[SM] is a leadership mindset. They are interdependent frameworks that build culture, drive sales and create disciples. My hope is that readers easily connect to the frameworks, find the content compelling and adopt The Culture of Commerce[SM] to achieve transformative outcomes.

Disclaimer: The stories and examples in the book are real, but names have been changed to protect the privacy of the parties involved.

CHAPTER 1

THE CUSTOMER PREVENTION CULTURE^{SM}
The Friction-Filled Customer Experience

"It's not the employer who pays the wages. Employers only handle the money … It is the customer who pays the wages." —Henry Ford, Founder, Ford Motor Company

n late 2000, I had accepted a sales management position for a manufacturing business serving the metal forming industry. I was responsible for the company's largest Midwest sales region, supervising four field sales reps and eight customer service people.

Of six regional sales managers covering North America, I was the youngest of the group. One of my colleagues, Don Duncan, was the eldest member of our team. He was responsible for Canada and based in Greater Toronto. When I informed Don that I was born in Canada, he responded, "That explains your manners and command of the English language." Don was nearing retirement and the 30-year gap between us was obvious in how he handled pressure and difficult situations. He'd seen it all and was unflappable. I was young, impatient and sometimes handled situations poorly.

The horrible events of 9/11 occurred about one year into the job, and my territory shrunk from $18 million to $11 million. As expected, what followed was an enormous amount of pressure to turn sales results around. Usually the pressure was delivered during our Monday morning sales call led by my boss, the VP of Sales. Although my colleagues felt some pressure, the VP seemed to direct more of it toward me, likely because I had the largest sales region and he'd brought me into the organization. The period following 9/11 was unlike anything I'd ever seen. The marketplace was at a standstill, and I questioned my team's ability to drive sales results.

At one point, I called Don to share a specific challenge where I wasn't getting support from an internal team on a new business opportunity. I'd encountered friction from this team a few times and needed a sanity check. I explained the situation, and after taking it all in, he laughed and said, "Tommy, didn't you know? They are known as *The Customer Prevention Department.* They've been doing this for as long as I can remember." I laughed out loud. He gave what I was experiencing a name, and I've never forgotten it. Since Don introduced me to the concept, I've renamed it The Customer Prevention Culture^{SM} because I've found the mindset to be systemic rather than isolated to a person, team or event. This is an important point to remember as you read further and reflect on your own work environment.

The Customer Prevention Culture^{SM} is intended to strike you as absurd. After all, who in their right mind would set out to build, foster or perpetuate a culture that prevents customers? Nobody! And yet, in my experience, it's pervasive throughout business. Heck, if you simply go about your day as a consumer, I'd be shocked if you didn't bump into The Customer Prevention Culture^{SM}.

I've owned and operated my own sales agency for 15 years, and during that time, my sales teams have represented 40 different companies. Ninety percent of the companies we've represented have struggled with The Customer Prevention Culture^{SM} in some form or fashion. The result has been the inability to sustainably generate organic growth. What does that look like? In my experience, it looks like businesses riding the highs and lows of economic cycles rather than creating a growth trajectory through hyper-focused customer acquisition and retention. If you're a commission-based salesperson, it's a challenging environment to endure. On many occasions I've been the lone voice willing to call out The Customer Prevention Culture^{SM}, only to realize my co-workers lacked the internal will to address it. How can this be? Well, I would argue that individuals working in The Customer Prevention Culture^{SM} are both lost and numb to the effects of their culture on the customer experience. They've checked out. They're desensitized because of a prolonged lack of leadership, vision and standards that's left them going through the motions.

Let me share a few stories that shed light on The Customer Prevention Culture^{SM}.

I Finally Broke Up With the U.S. Postal Service

I compare my relationship with my local U.S. Postal Service to Stockholm Syndrome. *Stockholm Syndrome is described as feelings of trust or affection felt in many cases of kidnapping or hostage-taking by a victim toward a captor.* I use the comparison because as a customer of the U.S. Postal Service, while being repeatedly abused, I somehow felt they were doing something good for me. They made me feel like I was the problem. The employees were miserable, rude and slow.

To make matters worse, they didn't realize it was their job to be the experts on the Post Office's incredibly confusing menu of services.

My typical interaction would begin with a very long line from the door to the counter. In their world, it's the customer's responsibility to choose which applicable service to use for their letter or package. Once the customer determines their desired service, they must find the exact form to correspond to the service, complete it and hand it to the clerk upon reaching the counter. Most of the time, I'd be informed by the clerk that I chose the wrong form, completed it incorrectly or the service I chose wasn't available for this package type or ship-to address. At that point, I'd be advised to step out of the line to correct my mistake. Of course, they'd say, "Once you complete the correct form, you can just step back up to the counter. You don't have to go to the back of the line." They're so nice! Now either I'm an idiot or they don't make it easy to do business with them. I'll spare you my rant on government-run institutions and what happens without competition, but the U.S. Postal Service is an epic example. About 10 years ago, I vowed never to set foot inside their facilities again, even if that meant paying five times the money to use expedited delivery services. Interestingly, my go-to sources make it so incredibly easy to do business, the only time I consider price is when I see the line item on my credit card statement. I've stayed true to my vow and, thankfully, ended my toxic relationship with my local U.S. Post Office.

Stranded at ABC Rent-a-Car

I had just returned home from a vacation in Florida. My wife and I enjoyed seven days in the sun with some longtime friends and had a blast. When you live in the Midwest, it's nice to escape the cold and break up the winter. When I booked flights for this trip the previous October, I also rented a car and made sure to use a service called *Getaway*. For me, customer experience in the car rental business is all about vehicle pickup, vehicle return and logistics to and from the airport. The car itself is almost meaningless.

Getaway allows the customer to go directly to the car and avoid standing in lines upon arrival.

It's always a great time when customers are greeted this way! Stranded at ABC Rent-a-Car.

To enroll in Getaway, the customer is required to set up a profile and provide a valid credit card and driver's license. Unfortunately, it was President's Week; Getaway should have been renamed *Stranded*. Customers were lined out the door when we were dropped off by the rental car shuttle. Adults were melting down in front of their kids. We watched as a mom of two used profanity that would make a truck driver blush. Customers were looking at a two-hour wait to get through the line and up to the counter. Clearly, this isn't how most people want to start their vacation.

ABC Rent-a-Car was understaffed, with a queue of returned vehicles to be cleaned and re-fueled before becoming available to new customers. How could ABC Rent-a-Car be caught flat-footed during one of the busiest vacation weeks of the year? Wouldn't it be reasonable to expect them to flag known school break weeks during the season so they could build rental car inventories, staff up and take full advantage of customer demand? The weekly rental rate I paid was at least 50% higher than normal, so the price reflected peak season. If the prices reflected peak season, why was the operation so ill-prepared? Fortunately for us, even though the paperwork and rental car weren't ready when we arrived, the line for Getaway customers was far shorter, so we were able to get in and out in less than 30 minutes — still not ideal, but I'll take my experience over the poor customers lined out the door.

Quit Cable? Think Again!

I've yet to cut the cord on conventional cable, but did take a slight detour last year when I fired my cable provider and hired a satellite company for both programming and internet service. Over the course of 12 months, I frequently lost the satellite signal and my internet service was horrible. What did I do? I went back to cable with my tail between my legs. Parting ways with the satellite company was civil, but because I didn't stay with them for the agreed-upon 24-month term, they hit me with a $200 early termination fee. The cancellation phone call got interesting.

Me: "Why can't you waive the early termination fee?"

Customer Care: "I'm sorry, sir, but we extended you a promotional rate based on a 24-month agreement."

Me: "You're right about the terms, but if I recall correctly from my business law class, a bind-ing contract requires both parties to live up to the agreement. I had service issues with the sat-ellite and even more so with internet, which is why I'm canceling service. Your company didn't deliver on your promise. Based on that information alone, doesn't it seem reasonable that you'd waive the early termination fee?"

Customer Care: "I understand where you're coming from, sir, but I show only one record of you calling to report trouble, and we never sent a tech to your home to investigate. Unless we've confirmed the issue by having a tech on-site, we have no basis to waive the termination fee."

Me: "Right, I never called because I didn't want to spend 45 minutes on the phone with your company being passed around the call center like a hot potato."

Customer Care: "I understand, sir, but I have no authority to waive the fee."

Me: "Got it. Here is what I'd like you to do: I want you to make a note in your system that I'm objecting to paying the early termination fee. Can you confirm you've done that?"

Customer Care: "Absolutely, sir, I've made a note that you object to paying the early termination fee."

Me: "Great. Thanks for your time and have a great day."

Customer Care: "Well, Mr. Halpin, we are sorry to see you go, but I do have one last question. Was I able to satisfactorily answer all of your questions today, and would you recommend Satellite TV to your friends and family?"

Me: "C'mon, man. Replay our conversation. You, personally, were fine, but I obviously didn't have a great experience with Satellite TV so, no, I wouldn't recommend your company to my friends and family."

Customer Care Representative: "I understand, sir. Thank you, and have a wonderful day."

I'll spare you the additional phone conversations that followed to clarify instructions on equipment return and billing questions. Nonetheless, I ended up eating the early termination fee, but I'm also convinced they could have kept me as a customer if I'd had confidence in their ability to overcome the quality of service I was experiencing. The worst part? I now have a satellite dish on my roof.

Rock Manufacturing – We Are Family

Rock is a manufacturer of tooling components used in the plastic mold industry. Their customers serve a variety of industries including automotive, office furniture, consumer products, appliances and more. Rock has at least three industry peers that would be considered leaders relative to product, quality and service. Rock is very much a follower and No. 4 in market share. I'd categorize Rock as a "lifestyle business" for its owner, which isn't a criticism, just a fact. For the last 20 years, he has been a passive owner, hired managers to run the business and enjoyed the free cashflow generated to support his lifestyle. In many ways, he is living the entrepreneurial dream. The owner, now enjoying retirement, started the business in a garage in 1974 and grew it to over $20 million with locations in the U.S., Canada, Spain and Mexico.

Rock has two primary customers: plastic injection molders and mold makers.

In North America, Rock has locations in London, Ontario, and Detroit, Michigan. London is both the corporate office and primary manufacturing hub with 100 employees, whereas Detroit has limited manufacturing capability, producing only simple parts with 15 employees. To sum up the relationship between the two plants, London is Detroit's supplier for just about everything.

Detroit places two types of orders with London — stock replenishment (blanks) and immediate customer requirements. Most everything Detroit manufactures is produced from a blank, a work-in-process inventory that allows Rock to finish to order quickly based on the customer's preferred dimensional requirements. Immediate customer requirements consist of complex products that Detroit does not have the capability to produce. When Detroit receives a customer order, they process a make-buy decision. If it makes sense to produce the part in Detroit, they will. If not, they source it to London. One hundred percent of Detroit's stock requirements are placed with London. As a result, Detroit is London's No. 1 customer. Granted they're an internal customer, but they are a customer nonetheless (more on that later). In short, Detroit is highly reliant on its supply relationship with London. Therein lies the problem.

Although Detroit is London's No. 1 customer, it's not treated that way. London views Detroit as the younger sibling who can be continually taken advantage of. Orders from Detroit can be late because, after all, they're family and where else can they go? If London has a backlog of Detroit orders, they will often arbitrarily process orders in a sequence of their choosing, rather than prioritizing based upon Detroit's needs.

Additionally, London quotes all of Detroit's complex work. Similar to manufacturing lead times, quote turnaround is highly inconsistent. Sometimes London supplies quotes in 24 hours, and at other times, it can take a week. Customers want answers, Detroit is caught in the middle and company resources get consumed in a cycle of futility.

London's approach to stock replenishment, immediate customer requirements and quote turnaround negatively affects Detroit's ability to provide a consistent customer experience.

This is a textbook example of the gaps that exist when internal people, teams or locations aren't viewed as customers.

These stories highlight specific experiences that are representative of a larger, systemic problem. In some cases, there is an absence of leadership and the business has been neglected. In other instances, team members are living out a lack of values and shared organizational outcomes. The takeaway is that culture is on display day to day, and leadership must establish a standard or team members are left to their own devices. Interestingly, all of the companies referenced previously have experienced some level of success. Each has a value proposition, provides gainful employment to many, creates profits for owners and shareholders and services a wide range of customers. They most certainly do many things right or they wouldn't be in business. However on the spectrum of The Customer Prevention Culture[SM] versus The Culture of Commerce[SM], a few of them need to reboot. Imagine their success if they were able to remove friction in their businesses. They'd have greater customer retention, separate themselves from the competition and increase the flow of commerce.

Companies suffering from The Customer Prevention Culture^SM exhibit some or all of the following patterns:

- A disjointed customer experience as customer touchpoints create friction and confusion. To the customer, few interactions are seamless, clean and without speed bumps.
- Organizational misalignment with tribes and silos. To the customer, it doesn't feel like a shared organizational outcome exists because the people and functional areas they interact with aren't on the same page.
- A company-centric infrastructure exists where people, process and technology are established to serve the needs of the company and internal stakeholders rather than the customer. To the customer, it feels like their vendor's systems, processes and business rules don't support and simplify commerce.
- Building culture is an afterthought rather than an active leadership mindset.
- The customer is not king!

For the customer, friction equates to pain that results from slowing down their desired pace of doing business with a supplier, vendor or service provider. Specific pain such as poor quality, lousy customer service and late delivery leaves the customer confused, frustrated and lacking confidence. The fallout that results is excessive customer turnover, salespeople working double duty to insulate customers from friction throughout the customer life cycle and suboptimized organizational resources. In the end, The Customer Prevention Culture^SM creates a customer experience that is more friction than flow. In this atmosphere, customers find doing business so painful they're forced to leave in search of a supplier that makes life easier.

The Customer Prevention Culture^SM is embodied by the following themes:

(See graphic on next page)

- Rigidity
- Lack of creativity
- Unproductive comfort zones
- Lack of problem-solving

These themes are indicative of leaders with fixed mindsets. *Fixed mindsets* and *growth mindsets* are both terms developed by Carol S. Dweck, Ph.D. People with fixed mindsets avoid challenges, have a fear of failure and believe intelligence is static. Fixed mindset folks avoid feedback, stop when challenges get too difficult and feel threatened by the success of others. Growth mindset people believe new abilities can be developed, view life as an exciting adventure and feel that anything can be learned. They celebrate trying and believe failure is part of learning and that problems present interesting challenges. I've been asked, *"What happens when you encounter clients hardwired for The Customer Prevention Culture^SM?"* It's pretty simple. I wish them well

The Customer Prevention Culture℠ – Presents Friction Throughout The Customer Life Cycle

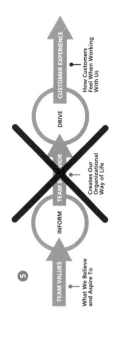

Customer Touchpoints Break Confidence

Verbal

Documentation

Physical

Troubleshooting

Digital

Call Center Support

Fulfillment

③

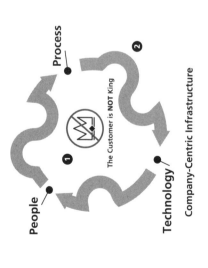

People

Process

①

The Customer is NOT King

Technology

②

Company-Centric Infrastructure

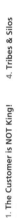

TEAM VALUES — What We Believe and Aspire To

INFORM

TEAM BEHAVIOR — Creates Our Organizational Way of Life

DRIVE

CUSTOMER EXPERIENCE — How Customers Feel When Working With Us

⑤

No Values to Form Culture

④

Tribes & Silos = Team Lacks Shared Organizational Outcomes

1. The Customer is NOT King!
2. Company-Centric Infrastructure
3. Customer Touchpoints Break Confidence
4. Tribes & Silos
5. No Values to Form Culture

The Customer Prevention Culture℠ is Embodied by the Following Principles:

THE**HALPIN**GROUP

©2019 The Halpin Group, LLC

and hope they eventually wake up to reality. If they don't believe change is needed, what can be done? Ultimately, folks hardwired for The Customer Prevention Culture^{SM} typically have fixed mindsets. Their choice is to change or eventually get left behind.

Leaders in The Customer Prevention Culture^{SM} typically exhibit the following traits:

A lack of humility. These leaders aren't interested in seeking out best practices, benchmarking or participating in networking forums to learn how industry peers are winning in the marketplace. Isolation is their common theme as opposed to joining learning communities where information-sharing is available to discover industry trends and the actions other companies are taking to improve their businesses.

A defensiveness and belief that their current state doesn't require change. No creativity or motivation to create new value for their customers. Leaders in The Customer Prevention Culture^{SM} like to coast by maintaining their businesses or jobs. *"If I can get five to ten more years out of this gig, that would be ideal"* would be typical of their thought process. Creating new value for customers runs contrary to their primary motivation of self-preservation. They prefer not to rock the boat. Risk-taking, championing new ideas or challenging status quo isn't in their makeup.

A general disregard of the real threats and disruptions they face in the marketplace. Disruption is when the status quo gets replaced by a better way of doing something and is validated by market adoption. For example, many businesses have been disrupted as a result of the internet. One such category is business directories like the Yellow Pages or The Thomas Register of American Manufacturers. For decades, people used directories for sourcing decisions or to search for businesses that met their needs. These directory businesses were disrupted when the internet made it possible for a company like Google to become an aggregator of information, making it easy for users to find businesses or conduct research with a simple keyword search. These are perfect examples of what happens when leaders are not forward-thinking and mindful of looming threats in the marketplace. Instead, they end up hanging on by their fingernails trying to make their old business models relevant while savvier businesses eat their lunch.

People aren't viewed as their greatest asset. Those practicing The Customer Prevention Culture^{SM} view people as transactional where having employees is obligatory. *"I need a certain number of people in these roles to have a minimum viable business, so we'll staff our business accordingly"* is their viewpoint. They fill positions, and since their culture is an afterthought, they're not mindful of aligning people with their culture. They employ a mechanical approach to the human resource function. Conversely, companies that view people as their greatest asset have a completely different approach. They believe talent drives the business and acquiring good people is not an accident. It's strategic. As a result, they recruit specific types of people that will flourish in their culture and develop them through coaching, mentorship, peer reviews and personal development plans.

A lack of interest in the customer's perspective to gain insights. Leaders in The Customer Prevention Culture^{SM} enjoy the secluded comforts of their office, where they can avoid the practicalities of the real world. Leaders practicing the opposite understand that customer insights help to shape a better future and put listening mechanisms in place to connect regularly and hear from them.

In your own work environment, do these leadership traits seem familiar?

The following scenario is playing out in organizations with alarming frequency.

Scenario: Internal Kickoff Meeting to Onboard a New Client

Context: The sales cycle has spanned 12 months, the salesperson has overcommunicated throughout the sales process and involved the appropriate team members to establish expectations prior to closing the deal. In short, the salesperson has without a doubt greased the skids of commerce!

No. 1 Salesperson: "I've got good news, everyone. We sold the deal!"

Operations Team: "Oh man, that's awesome. Congrats. Wait, not to be a downer, but how are we going to deliver? We better review our resources to make sure we can fulfill the project deliverables."

Project Management: "Salesperson No. 1, I know we discussed this project briefly, but the timeline seems awfully aggressive. We'll need to review the scope of work to see if this is even doable. Also, we're unclear on some of the customer's requirements, so we'll need to address them right away."

Finance: "Did we quote this properly? The margins look tight."

Sales Leader: "Good job, No. 1! Go sell another one, but we may need to discuss your comp plan."

If you're reading the exchange above thinking, *This is standard operating procedure in my organization; what's the big deal?* I'd respond in this way: Customer-centric teams welcome challenging projects and are committed to finding a way to deliver. They value new customer relationships and have an appreciation for what goes into selling them. The collective tone above is discouraging if you happen to be salesperson No. 1 because he sold the deal, communicated thoroughly and now his team has amnesia. It takes a special salesperson to endure this repeatedly, and yet many salespeople will tell you closing a deal is only the beginning of their process. In many environments, selling internally consumes as much time as selling externally.

Keep in mind, the scenario above is symptomatic of The Customer Prevention Culture^{SM} because, if the customer onboarding process begins this way, I guarantee additional constraints to commerce will surface downstream.

The Customer Prevention Culture^{SM} is a disease, and when allowed to persist, it spreads. To remedy the disease, leaders must be willing to call out The Customer Prevention Culture^{SM} when encountering it and then teach their team to adopt a higher standard by introducing The Culture of Commerce^{SM}.

THE CULTURE OF COMMERCE^{SM}
The Remedy for Customer Prevention Culture^{SM}

CHAPTER **2**

"For individuals, character is destiny. For organizations,
culture is destiny." —Tony Hsieh, CEO, Zappos

'm on a mission to call out The Customer Prevention Culture^{SM} wherever it's found and provide the remedy: The Culture of Commerce^{SM}. It's true that no company intentionally sets out to build a Customer Prevention Culture^{SM}, but it inevitably creeps its way into people, process and technology. This results in friction, making it difficult for customers to do business.

As a sales leader and consultant, I've come to realize The Customer Prevention Culture^{SM} is rampant throughout the B2B marketplace and in desperate need of eradicating. When allowed to exist, The Customer Prevention Culture^{SM} makes it nearly impossible to grow a business because company resources are misaligned, resulting in poor customer experience and excessive customer turnover. The goal of this book is to shed light on The Customer Prevention Culture^{SM}, educate readers on The Culture of Commerce^{SM} and outline a plan for mass adoption for those that find it compelling.

Today, we hear the term customer experience daily. However, to impact customer experience, there must be an underlying culture to support it. In my mind, this hinges on leaders equipping their teams to honestly assess how people, process and technology affect every customer touchpoint throughout the customer life cycle. The Culture of Commerce^{SM} enables the entire team to participate and buy into a larger vision by educating them on five foundational principles while providing the tools necessary to eliminate The Customer Prevention Culture^{SM} within specific workflows. The Culture of Commerce^{SM} is both powerful and necessary for organizations to thrive. I hope you decide to join me on the mission!

The Culture of Commerce^{SM} stomps out the incongruency so pervasive in business culture today and is founded on the following principles:

1. The Customer is King!
2. Customer-Centric Infrastructure – People, Process and Technology
3. One Team – One Goal
4. All Customer Touchpoints Build Confidence
5. Values Form Culture

Let's break down each of the five principles. *(See graphic on next page)*

The Customer is King!

Yes, it's true. The customer is king, can buy from whomever they'd like and their business is the reward for companies that serve them best. "The customer is king" is one of the tenets of free enterprise. It's not a new idea. However, it appears to be lost on most companies given the consistent amount of friction in customer experience at-large. Across industries, the pursuit and onboarding of new customers is overemphasized while post-customer acquisition activities are de-emphasized. And, oh by the way, strong customer service is the exception rather than the rule — all of which are constraints to organic growth because it becomes difficult to build a customer base, nurture relationships and retain them.

Years ago, when my kids were 3 and 5 years old, we decided to take them to a water park outside of Cleveland. After being in the park for less than an hour, my wife and I realized we had made a mistake. Most of the activities had height requirements, but rather than having a stationary measuring stick prominently visible as you entered the activity, the water park had employees walking around with the measuring stick, sometimes after children had already entered the activity area. You can imagine the outcome. The taller child enters the activity with the younger, shorter child. One gets to stay and enjoy the activity and the other is told they're too short, forced to leave dejected and crying. It was beyond idiotic. After this happened twice, my wife said, "Stay here with the kids. I'm going to see if we can get our money back."

After no sign of my wife for 30 minutes, she called me from her cell phone and asked me to bring the kids up to the park entrance. There I found her surrounded by college-age park employees. "What's up?" I said.

The Culture of Commerce℠ - The Remedy For The Customer Prevention Culture℠

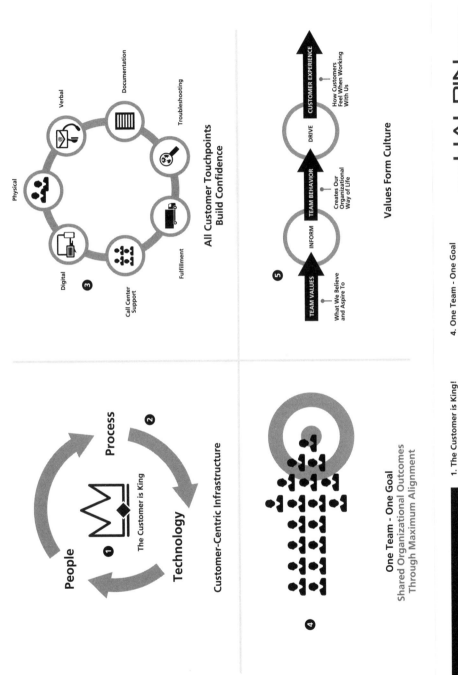

People

Process

Technology

The Customer is King

① Customer-Centric Infrastructure

Physical

Verbal

Documentation

Troubleshooting

Digital

Call Center Support

Fulfillment

③ All Customer Touchpoints Build Confidence

One Team - One Goal
Shared Organizational Outcomes Through Maximum Alignment

④

TEAM VALUES — What We Believe and Aspire To

INFORM

TEAM BEHAVIOR — Creates Our Organizational Way of Life

DRIVE

CUSTOMER EXPERIENCE — How Customers Feel When Working With Us

⑤ Values Form Culture

The Culture of Commerce℠ is Founded on the Following Principles:

1. The Customer is King!
2. Customer-Centric Infrastructure
3. All Customer Touchpoints Build or Break Confidence
4. One Team - One Goal
5. Values Form Culture

THE**HALPIN**GROUP
©2019 The Halpin Group, LLC

My wife explained, "They're telling me they can't refund our money but will give us vouchers to come back. I told them I really don't want to come back and we don't live in the area." After reasoning with the manager, they agreed to refund our money and we departed for another amusement park nearby.

Looking back, the customer clearly wasn't king. But perhaps the water park hadn't considered who their customer was. It was plain to me the water park was serving families with an emphasis on children. Those of us with kids know that if they're happy, everyone is happy, and if we're going to a water park, it's surely about them. With that end in mind, the water park could have created a much stronger customer experience. They missed it in a big way. We never returned.

In too many organizations, customers are treated like a nuisance rather than a king. Too often it's as if team members are unaware that, if not for customers, there is no opportunity for a business to thrive, profit, reinvest, expand, develop new products and provide advancement opportunities, all of which result from a growing enterprise. Embracing *The Customer is King!* is the cornerstone of The Culture of Commerce^{SM} and sets the stage for the remaining principles.

Customer-Centric Infrastructure – People, Process and Technology

Since the customer is king, it follows that customer-driven firms take their most valuable resources — people, process and technology — and deploy them in a customer-centric fashion. I've found that people are often misplaced, misaligned and frustrated, with poor attitudes that leak out into customer interactions. Too often it feels as though enterprises are enslaved to processes and technology that don't serve the customer and therefore create frictional commerce.

Companies aspiring to achieve a customer-centric infrastructure should beware of the following customer prevention mindsets and patterns:

- "We've always done it this way" or "This is the way we do it" is indicative of a lazy team mindset that's given up on continuous improvement.
- "We cannot produce that customer report from the ERP (enterprise resource planning) system today and it would require custom code to generate." This is symptomatic of The Customer Prevention Culture^{SM} and technology being master over the needs of the business. Why have an ERP system that doesn't provide team members with basic actionable information? Remember: Access to timely information can be a competitive advantage.
- "We can't close this customer request because Reggie is out." This is indicative of a single team member so central to a workflow that a process, transaction or output cannot be completed without their involvement. How can one person bring a process to a halt?

There are a host of other examples, but you get the point. People, process and technology need to be deployed around the customer to facilitate commerce. To do otherwise makes life overly difficult for everyone involved, especially the customer. A bonus to the customer-centric infrastructure principle is that enterprise resources are optimized to drive productivity and profits. It's a no-brainer.

One Team – One Goal

One Team – One Goal requires leaders and team members to be singularly focused and aligned to achieve shared organizational outcomes. For that to become reality, leadership teams must be honest enough to acknowledge their people-based constraints and organizational misalignment. A major misconception is that only customer-facing functions and positions need be reviewed, but this is shortsighted. Why? Because 100% of team members and functions must be viewed as customer-impacting. If not, why employ them?! As an example, is a customer service team member more important than a fulfillment center worker? Their duties are interdependent, which is why the singularly focused team is crucial to achieving a positive, sustainable customer experience.

Additionally, all companies need to teach their team that we all have customers, internal or external. If we view the people and teams upstream and downstream of us as customers, we develop a more thoughtful mindset.

Let's further explore people-based constraints and organizational misalignment.

Meet Phil

In team environments, we've all run into a guy like Phil, the maverick information-hoarding guy who wants to be a lone wolf. He thinks hoarding information is job security and doesn't work well in teams. For over a decade, I've worked with Phil through one of my principals. He is incredible in many ways. He is super smart, has great rapport with customers, is hard-working and will do anything to support new business opportunities. We've grown our respective businesses significantly since working together. In many ways, Phil is the dream. He behaves like an owner, even though he is not. What's interesting about Phil is that many of his traits are applauded in American culture. Let's face it, we embrace bootstrappers, independence, leadership and autonomy. Phil possesses all of these attributes, but for me, Phil is the problem performer. He's awesome and takes great pride in his work, but it all falls apart because he thinks he's bigger than the enterprise. That, my friends, is a deal breaker.

If Phil is in the mix, it's impossible to transfer his knowledge to other employees, build out talent on the team and share work, all of which are critical to grow and serve more customers. When Phil is out of the office, the business begins to break down. Customer quotes pile up, job status updates are unavailable and spare parts can't be shipped. Customers get responses like, "I'm sorry, but you'll have to wait until Monday when Phil gets back from vacation." If you have one key team member or several team members like Phil, the singular focus of one team, one goal is hard to achieve. That's why Phil needs to adapt or move on. If not, it becomes impossible to multiply influence and build a team.

Organizational Misalignment – Tribes & Silos Versus One Cohesive Unit

Within companies, it's common to see different functional areas and teams operating in silos. These silos operate as distinct operating units within a larger enterprise. The silo effect inherently sets the stage for organizational misalignment because it encourages tribalism versus unification, knowingly or unknowingly. Tribalism is the state of fact of being organized in a tribe. Unification is the process of being united or made into a whole. As work flows from one tribe to another, friction surfaces, slowing down commerce. The leadership mindset associated with The Culture of Commerce^{SM} declares, "The customer should never sense the existence of tribes because we're one team – one goal and customer-centric." As an example, if the customer has relationships several people deep at a key vendor's company, that's a good thing. But if the customer is forced to navigate personalities and misalignment within a vendor organization because of disparate mindsets, values and attitudes, that makes for a bad situation. Another example is organizational team members working independently and autonomously rather than interdependently. A unified culture always wins the day, which is why One Team – One Goal is so huge.

Many years ago, I worked for a multinational company in the metals industry. They had a Michigan-based distribution center, and at times their warehouse manager was straight-up rogue. He was highly respected because of his time, tenure and contributions to the company as it'd grown from a small organization into a middle-market powerhouse. But when his boss or visitors from corporate would come to town, they'd affectionately refer to the Michigan distribution center as "Smith Enterprises," referring to the warehouse manager's last name. It was common for them to tour the distribution center only to stumble upon new equipment that he'd purchased without their knowledge or approval.

From my side it was hilarious, but looking back, not ideal. Smith would regularly reallocate budget to do what he felt was necessary to support the business. It's been said there are two sides to every story and then the truth. Smith's side of the story was that his friends at corporate didn't understand the priorities of the distribution center, so it was up to him alone to make things happen. Corporate's side of the story was that they knew best and expected Smith to either stick with the plan or at least involve them in his newly hatched endeavors. The truth was likely that corporate leadership failed to communicate a shared vision with the team, which may have given Smith visibility into enterprise-wide priorities. This would have resulted in greater collaboration and the ability to work toward essential, shared organizational outcomes as One Team – One Goal.

The bottom line: Organizational misalignment is a failure of leadership to create vision that breaks down silos and tribes in their own companies. Look for rogue operators working in tribes and use The Culture of Commerce^{SM} to move toward unification. Remember that rogue operators are sometimes sabotage artists, and at other times, well-intentioned people who simply need coaching to get aligned with the team.

All Customer Touchpoints Build or Break Confidence

The perfect customer experience is all flow, no friction. In an "all flow" environment, customers have the ability to conduct business within different functional areas effortlessly throughout the customer life cycle. Those companies practicing the opposite — what I call The Customer Prevention Culture^{SM} — present unintentional friction throughout the customer life cycle. Adopters of The Culture of Commerce^{SM} understand selling the customer is not a one-time event. You don't sell the customer, onboard them and then it's over. Customer relationships are nurtured over time and grow as trust and credibility are established. This happens as customers interact with different team members throughout the organization. Common interactions and touchpoints include customer service, technical support, fulfillment, sales, quality, accounts receivable and many more. All customer touchpoints build or break confidence and back up the point that ALL team members have customer-impacting positions (customer-facing and non-customer facing).

Stated differently, and don't miss this point: We all have a customer!

It's been said that a customer problem, when handled well, actually creates more trust and confidence than if the issue had never happened. I am a believer in this simple truth!

I have an SUV and use the dealer for all maintenance. I take advantage of its shuttle service to get to and from my house so that I don't need to inconvenience my wife for pickups and drop-offs. All in all, the dealership provides very good service. Are the employees perfect? No. But it's clear the team is highly focused on customer service. My customer experience with the dealership has involved several touchpoints: the original vehicle purchase, online payment, ongoing maintenance and its shuttle service. I rank the shuttle service and ongoing vehicle maintenance as the key touchpoints because I interface with them every three to four months, which keeps me in front of them.

A few examples of the dealer touchpoints are as follows:

- Original Vehicle Purchase – The salesperson and sales manager were great, helped me quickly select a vehicle and I enjoyed working with them. However, the vehicle paperwork process took four to five hours of my life, and I want my time back. They need to reevaluate their systems and process. In a perfect world, I would handle the entire process online or via phone and then pick up the vehicle when ready.
- Infotainment Training – When I was tossed the keys, they had an employee jump in the

passenger seat to provide a quick tutorial on the vehicle infotainment system. This was a nice touch. He did a really thorough job, and I left appreciating the thoughtfulness of the interaction.

- Prepaid Maintenance Plan – I decided to purchase a vehicle maintenance plan that's good through 125,000 miles. It covers oil changes, brakes, wipers, air filters, tire rotations and other planned maintenance. During one maintenance session, the service writer called to advise me that I needed my cabin filter replaced. To my surprise, it wasn't covered in the maintenance plan. I challenged it. How could that be? If it's a predictable maintenance item that will need to be replaced, why wouldn't it be covered? I called my salesperson, who went to bat for me and covered the cabin filter replacement at no charge. In turn, they gained customer loyalty in me. They obviously need to address this issue at a higher level so that items with predictable maintenance are covered in the maintenance plan, however.

- Maintenance – I drop my car off at the dealership and then take the shuttle service back to the house and then again to pick up my car when service is complete. The shuttle service keeps me productive so I'm not losing excessive amounts of time to service my car. As a small business owner, I'm highly sensitive to my time being violated!

- Payment – I financed the vehicle and set up automatic bill payment through their online portal. The portal is easy to use with lots of information and provides optional automated updates for maintenance.

These are examples of customer touchpoints that serve to build or break confidence. I'm loyal to the dealership because their team does a really nice job servicing me. Because they're responsive and clearly focused on creating a strong customer experience, they've earned my confidence … for now. To lose my business, the dealer would have to completely lose their way or the OEM would have to produce really bad vehicles.

Examples of B2B customer touchpoints that build confidence include the following:

- A frictionless e-commerce buying experience where a new customer visits a company website, executes a product search, locates the product of interest, sees that it's in stock and transacts with a credit card. The buyer receives an email confirmation of the order, is notified when it ships, receives a tracking number and the order arrives on the buyer's shipping dock as promised. When the package is opened, the product is exactly what was ordered and ready for use.

- A manufacturer has a bad string of equipment failures in their plant and, based on their backlog of customer orders, determines they need to proactively notify customers that they'll be late because of unplanned equipment downtime. Leadership meets to review their entire open order report, determines when their equipment will be back online and feeds that information with revised ship dates to their customer service team. The customer service team calls the affected customers to advise them of the situation and provide the revised ship dates. Although some customers are negatively impacted by the late shipments, most are appreciative of the proactive notification from customer service.

- A software consulting firm, 12 months into a multiyear project, is advised by their customer that a glitch has been discovered in their software integration, and it's causing user experience issues on the customer's e-commerce site. It's alarming the customer, and their leadership team is requesting answers. The software consulting firm quickly identifies the root cause and builds a plan to fix the issue programmatically and communicates this back to the customer with a timeline to completion. The plan is executed quickly and the customer's confidence is restored.

- In a complex, multimillion-dollar sales cycle where one team is selling to another team, face-to-face meetings take place, web conferences are attended and presentations are shared with the prospect over a period of months. The sales cycle moves through the *education and exploration (Sales Zone No. 1), fit (Sales Zone No. 2)* and *decision-making zones (Sales Zone No. 3)*. In Sales Zone No. 1, the sellers first understand the client's desired business outcome in context and ask clarifying questions to gather additional data. Armed with that information, the seller educates the client and demonstrates leadership and authority in their space throughout all three sales zones and is ultimately awarded the business. How a company sells matters, and strong sales teams build confidence throughout the sales process. We will discuss the three sales zones in-depth later.

These are just a few examples of how different customer touchpoints build confidence. You'll notice some of these examples had the potential to break confidence, but when handled thoughtfully and responsively, they end up building confidence instead.

I encourage teams to examine all customer touchpoints whether physical, digital, verbal or written, including the inputs and outputs of the interaction like documentation supplied to customers. Auditing whether touchpoints build or break customer confidence is important to build culture, drive sales and create disciples.

Values Form Culture

I recently participated in a yearlong leadership process with eight other individuals and met weekly to review and discuss the study materials. During one weekly session, we spent time identifying our personal values. The study provided a starter list of values, and participants were encouraged to circle those that applied to them. Right on cue, I began circling values that resonated with me. As a next step, we were told something could only be a value if there was evidence of it in your life. If the value was something you aspired to, it was considered an ideal — not a value. It was a good exercise, because it forced me to reconcile reality with aspirational feelings. I really think this idea — values versus ideals — is relevant to culture because we often think something to be true that isn't. We think values exist, but when pressed for evidence, we come up empty.

To build culture, values need to be explained, taught and modeled to the team. For customer experience to be transformed, the enterprise's values need to support the customer experience they'd like to deliver. This may sound abstract, but I think we'd all agree every company has its own distinct personality — sometimes good and sometimes bad. That collective personality is their culture, and it penetrates every part of the business. More importantly, values and culture affect how the customer feels when interacting with your company.

In a family, it makes sense to discuss values, so everyone involved can understand this is what we believe and why, what we aren't willing to compromise and the outcomes we expect if we stay true to these values. Discussing values is important because it provides guiding principles and a standard to reference throughout life. However, I'd suggest that when they're lived out in plain view, they become real and much more likely to be adopted. The same is true in business. Talk is cheap until it's walked out, especially by those in positions of influence. Without defined values, we're aimlessly going about life and every day becomes an adventure, both individually and collectively. With no standard, people make choices and decisions on the fly, which is a recipe for disaster in the worst case and inconsistency in the best case. More importantly, it's no way to build a rock-solid culture. If you're serious about building The Culture of Commerce^{SM}, values matter!

The entire point of "values form culture" is to foster a consistently positive customer experience companywide by gaining mass adoption from the team. To really make that happen, companies need to determine how they want customers to feel while interacting with their people, process and technology throughout the customer life cycle.

What's your WHY? Understanding your WHY will uncover your values! Simon Sinek said, "People don't buy what you do, but why you do it. The goal is to do business with people who believe what you believe." Your values should support your WHY. My WHY is "to help clients transform their businesses through new mindsets, frameworks and implementation strategies."

For example, I want my clients to feel important, educated and impacted when working with me. Together, we get aligned on a shared business outcome and implement a plan to get there. I also want clients to feel a change in their condition after working with me. If our engagement is an event, I've failed. My values are rapport, resourcefulness, responsiveness and action orientation. What are your values? Are they merely words that decorate a whiteboard, or is there evidence to support they're real? More importantly, how will those values translate to how customers feel when they interact throughout the customer life cycle? If we miss this incredibly important point, we're wasting our time!

Recap

I've made my living owning and operating an independent sales agency for the last 15 years. We're an outsourced sales solution made up of a small team of salespeople, representing eight to 10 different companies selling throughout the U.S. at any given time. The 10% of my clients that are successful in consistently fulfilling their promises have a common theme: They believe the salesperson's role is to bring new customers into the fold and the internal team's job is to keep them. To help their internal team successfully retain customers, their leaders support them with continual education, monitoring and coaching. They believe that the right people, properly placed, have the greatest impact on growth. They also align compensation with team achievement of key performance indicators (KPIs) they believe to be growth drivers of their business. Lastly, their cultural standards and expectations transition from a leadership mindset to a team mindset quickly and consistently. It certainly makes sense that cultural aspirations begin as a leadership mindset, but if that's where it remains, it's all just window dressing.

Let's walk through an example of one company that, from personal experience, most closely tracks with The Culture of Commerce^{SM}.

Ace Manufacturing, St. Louis, Mo.

When I was first introduced to Ace Manufacturing, I noticed there was something very different about the organization. I'd come from a competitor that was 10 times their size and was interested to see how they stacked up. My first meeting was with Patrick Day, Managing Partner. Patrick shamelessly promoted his team and outlined the service-level standards he'd established for the company and his vision for growth. I don't consider myself a skeptic but did think, *"Is this guy for real? Or is he blowing smoke?"* I was meeting with him to discuss representing Ace Manufacturing in Michigan. After coming to terms, I soon learned what my customers would eventually experience. Their team was even better than Patrick had communicated. What followed was the fastest growth I'd experienced in any one relationship since starting my firm.

It was immediately clear that their inside sales team cared a lot. They genuinely appreciated the effort required to sell and onboard a new customer. Rather than turning around quotes in hours, which was typical of the industry, Ace Manufacturing generated quotes in minutes. When I met with their operations people, it was obvious they too were hyper-focused on serving customers, both new and existing. In conversations with their shop foreman, he'd ask me about specific customers and was obviously far more engaged than his counterparts at other companies I represented. There was a buzz in the air — both in the office and in the plant. The cherry on top was Patrick making aggressive investments to increase capacity to serve more customers. Simply put, Patrick was walking his talk. This business philosophy was validated by the growth Ace Manufacturing was experiencing.

Since their inception, Ace Manufacturing had sold entirely through direct salespeople, and my firm was their first attempt at using independent manufacturers' representatives. As a result of our relationship, Ace Manufacturing proceeded to hire additional manufacturers' rep agencies all over the country, with great success.

In looking at the Ace Manufacturing story, there are a few really important takeaways.

First, their pay structure aligns their team and rewards specific behavior. Their manufacturers' rep partners were paid a percentage of gross margin. This pay structure motivates reps to pursue profitable business rather than low-margin accounts. Their inside sales team compensation plan is a blend of base salary and variable compensation. The variable component pools a percentage of their gross margin dollars and distributes it to their entire team monthly. This pay structure motivates the inside team to nurture opportunities to grow the business one order and account at a time. Direct salespeople are paid a base salary plus commission. Finally, the shop participates in a profit-sharing plan paid out monthly. All parties were aligned toward the shared outcomes of sales, gross margin dollars and profit.

Second, Patrick Day sets high standards and is relentless with the team until they're adopted. Whether it be quote turnaround, lead time, customer care or quality, he refuses to accept mediocrity. He and his leadership team actively lead the business and hold the entire team accountable to the standards they believe will grow the business.

Third, the Ace Manufacturing team is highly customer-centric. Let me share a few examples. Their information technology (IT) was built to support core customer transactions and activity, rather than catering to internal stakeholders. Their IT makes it easy to quote customers, enter an order, send an order confirmation or group like orders for processing on the shop floor. If Ace is going to be late on a shipment, they notify the customer immediately and do their best to get partial shipments out the door based on customer priority. They're excited when the sales team brings in a new account. After the first shipment to a new customer, I'd frequently get a phone call from Patrick and this would be the exchange:

Patrick: "Tom, make sure to call XYZ Industries and ask them to share their reaction to the first shipment they received from Ace Manufacturing. Make sure to ask them about our quality compared to their previous vendor. By the way, Tom, do you know why I want you to ask?"

Me: "No. Why?"

Patrick: "Because, one, I know our quality is superior to the competition's and, two, I want the customer to hear themselves saying the words, 'Yes, we're very happy with the first shipment and the surface finish is far better than our previous vendor.' That's very important, Tom. I want them to hear the words roll off their tongue."

Then he'd laugh and tell me he should be a sales trainer.

I'm not suggesting Ace Manufacturing is perfect. They're not. What I am suggesting is they practice The Culture of Commerce^{SM} because they're hyper-focused on making it easy for customers to do business. They produce very little friction in the customer experience, and when friction does come up, it's isolated rather than systemic. The Ace Team is aligned, their compensation drives the right behavior and they have very high standards, all of which can be traced back to strong leadership.

Today, Ace Manufacturing continues to grow and recently completed a building expansion that doubled the size of their operations. Of the 40 businesses I've represented in 15 years, Ace Manufacturing most closely tracks with The Culture of Commerce^{SM}.

The Culture of Commerce^{SM} is built on the five principles we've explored in this chapter, but customers will experience the company's personality through different touchpoints — even in different mediums. The graphic on the next page illustrates where and how adopters of The Culture of Commerce^{SM} interface with customers throughout the customer life cycle.

(See graphic on next page)

If elements of The Customer Prevention Culture^{SM} exist in your business, identify friction points in the customer life cycle by addressing problematic workflows in your organization. The infographic found later in this chapter calls out the workflow by name, customer inputs (if applicable), enterprise outputs and resulting KPIs (actual versus goal), and then isolates the friction point by attributing if people, processes or technology are causing the constraint. The workflow is then priority-ranked based on return on investment or the quantifiable impact to the business.

Most friction is caused by suboptimized people, processes and technology. The goal is to reduce friction and increase flow through the smarter allocation of people, processes and technology to enable commerce. Those companies that make life easy for the customer win by building customer confidence and fostering The Culture of Commerce^{SM}. Keep in mind that a workflow may have a direct KPI or indirect KPI, since it might affect another process or customer upstream or downstream. A common mistake in The Customer Prevention Culture^{SM} is being unaware that all people or teams serve a customer, internally or externally. Adoption of this simple mindset has the potential to produce huge impact quickly.

Rock Manufacturing, Continued

Earlier, you learned about Rock Manufacturing and their facilities in London and Detroit. London is not only Detroit's primary source for both stock and complex customer parts, but it also quotes all of Detroit's complex work. As a result, Detroit's ability to fulfill customer commitments hinges upon London's on-time delivery performance, quality and quote turnaround. Since Detroit is London's No. 1 customer, it's important they develop a KPI scorecard to create alignment,

The Culture of Commerce℠ – Delivering a Frictionless Customer Experience

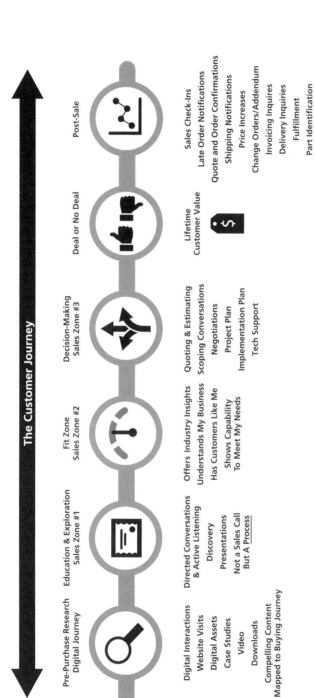

The Customer Journey

| Pre-Purchase Research
Digital Journey | Education & Exploration
Sales Zone #1 | Fit Zone
Sales Zone #2 | Decision-Making
Sales Zone #3 | Deal or No Deal | Post-Sale |

Digital Interactions
Website Visits
Digital Assets
Case Studies
Video
Downloads
Compelling Content
Mapped to Buying Journey

Directed Conversations
& Active Listening
Discovery
Presentations
Not a Sales Call
But A Process

Offers Industry Insights
Understands My Business
Has Customers Like Me
Shows Capability
To Meet My Needs

Quoting & Estimating
Scoping Conversations
Negotiations
Project Plan
Implementation Plan
Tech Support

Lifetime
Customer Value

Sales Check-Ins
Late Order Notifications
Quote and Order Confirmations
Shipping Notifications
Price Increases
Change Orders/Addendum
Invoicing Inquires
Delivery Inquiries
Fulfillment
Part Identification
Ease of Use/Application

Points To Ponder: Customer Touchpoints Offer The Potential to Build or Break Confidence.
Friction is Bad & Flow is Good! How Does Your Company Rate?

drive accountability and link the interdependencies of their workflows. A published KPI scorecard increases visibility for all stakeholders. The following represents meaningful KPIs for the Rock Manufacturing London-to-Detroit relationship.

Rock Manufacturing Scorecard
London to Detroit

	Goal	Actual
Quote Turnaround	4 hours	8 hours
On-Time Delivery	95%	70%
Stock Replenishment Lead time	4 weeks	12 weeks
Immediate Customer Requirement	Lead Time Negotiable Per Order	
Reject Rate @ Line Item	0%	1%

Rock Manufacturing Detroit has lost customers and sacrificed growth because their supplier refused to see them as a customer. We all have internal or external customers — our workflows are interconnected and they all impact customer experience. Identify the KPIs your team affects and work together with customers upstream or downstream to build a relationship. Too often, we're isolated in tribes and silos rather than working as one team with one goal. Often leaders must remove cultural barriers and establish new expectations in order for teams to work toward shared organizational outcomes.

Do-It-Yourself Truck Rental
Recently I called a truck rental company to reserve a one-way rental to take furniture to a cottage I'd purchased. I live in the Detroit area and was hoping to pick up a 20-foot truck close to home. I booked the rental while driving and the customer service rep emailed a confirmation to my smartphone. Upon arriving home, I opened the confirmation only to learn the truck pickup was in Canada! (I don't live in Canada, by the way.) This was obviously a mistake. I ended up spending 40 minutes on three different phone calls before finally resolving the issue.

If they did it to me, it's likely happening at many branches throughout their company. I can tell you the truck rental company needs The Culture of Commerce[SM] in a big way. If we think of this simple transaction as a workflow, we could begin to break down a solution. Their customer service KPIs might include customer satisfaction scores, one-call transactions, multi-call transactions and average transaction size. Their ability to execute one-call transactions would be a positive indicator of customer experience. Multiple phone calls would be an indicator of poor customer experience. Average transaction size and customer satisfaction scores would be higher in stores with better salespeople, producing better overall customer experience. Customer satisfaction scores would also provide a feedback mechanism to get better.

(See graphic on next page)

The practical steps teams can take to begin implementing The Culture of Commerce[SM] include the following:

1. All Customer Touchpoints Build or Break Confidence

    a. Identify problematic workflows that choke commerce. Look for workflows with excessive friction and isolate the KPI being affected directly or indirectly. If a KPI doesn't exist, create one in order to heighten visibility and quantify the impact. This is critical to priority-rank workflows based on the quantifiable impact to the organization. Talk to your customers! Share what you're up to and ask them what it's like to be on the customer side of the relationship. What's it like to be in their shoes? Don't make the mistake of trying to identify problematic workflows in isolation. It won't end well.

    b. As workflows are reviewed, look for patterns in people, process and technology to determine which components of the infrastructure are contributing to friction. When common themes present themselves across functional areas, the opportunity to remove friction across multiple touchpoints can create momentum and productivity to the enterprise quickly. Typically, leadership will assign cross-functional teams with unique skill sets to a given workflow depending on the contributing factors causing the constraint. For example, if technology is creating friction, it would be important to have the IT team involved to collaborate with users who live in that workflow.

2. One Team – One Goal

    a. Identify tribes and silos that exist in specific teams or functional areas. People are all incredibly different, with both strengths and weaknesses. It's a reality that rogue operators and sabotage artists do exist, but for the most part, I believe people want to do a good job. In the end, it's unproductive to assign motives to people, teams and functional areas when tribes and silos are identified. It's far more productive to educate and discuss shared organizational outcomes and how their buy-in is critical for maximizing alignment and advancing The Culture of Commerce[SM]. We often hear the term "peer pressure" in a negative context. I believe adoption of The Culture of Commerce[SM] creates a constructive form of peer pressure among team members by building accountability throughout the enterprise.

The Culture of Commerce℠ Diagnostic – Identifying Friction in The Customer Life Cycle

	DESCRIPTION	GOAL KPI	ACTUAL KPI	LIMITING INFRASTRUCTURE	QUANTITATIVE IMPACT	QUALITATIVE IMPACT	PRIORITY 1-5
WORKFLOW 1				☐ PEOPLE ☐ PROCESS ☐ TECHNOLOGY			
WORKFLOW 2				☐ PEOPLE ☐ PROCESS ☐ TECHNOLOGY			
WORKFLOW 3				☐ PEOPLE ☐ PROCESS ☐ TECHNOLOGY			
WORKFLOW 4				☐ PEOPLE ☐ PROCESS ☐ TECHNOLOGY			

3. Build a Training Plan

    a. The Culture of Commerce^{SM} requires continuous education over time to gain team adoption. The five principles need to be taught, explained and incorporated into the company's management system. Additionally, Values Form Culture needs to be established by company leadership. Values are unique to each company and should be messaged, modeled and taught to the entire organization. As the principle states, team values form team behavior, which ultimately drives the customer experience.

    b. Adoption of The Culture of Commerce^{SM} requires a transition from leadership mindset to team mindset. Remember: If it's just a leadership mindset, what's the point? Team adoption multiplies influence by equipping people with a new standard through which to view the customer experience, company culture and the infrastructure supporting the business. As teams are enlightened on how customer experience is affected by friction versus flow, they become more mindful of the people, process and technology they interact with and the effects on customer touchpoints. By understanding how infrastructure shapes commerce, they begin to think and behave like owners of process rather than passive participants.

4. KPIs — Establish, Monitor & Adjust

    a. Review team KPIs by introducing the philosophy that everyone has a customer, whether internal or external. Once it's understood that team KPIs can be affected by functional areas upstream or downstream, it reveals the interdependency of the organization. For example, data entry in customer service affects the fulfillment team in the warehouse, which affects the accounts receivable team. How? As an example, incorrect order entry in customer service could cause fulfillment to pick and pack the wrong item, impacting the accounts receivable group to collect payment. The point is our workflows all connect.

    b. KPIs should be revisited to ensure they aren't meaningless metrics. I suggest putting KPIs through three filters:

    1. Determine the most important drivers of company growth.

    2. Talk to your most forward-thinking customers and capture their expectations of vendors, suppliers and service providers. What's most meaningful to the customer and how can your company help them achieve their business goals?

    3. Test KPIs against The Culture of Commerce^{SM} framework. After weighing existing KPIs against these three filters, do they remain relevant or need modification?

These are four practical steps companies can take to begin implementing The Culture of Commerce^{SM} today.

For the remainder of this book, we'll focus on The Sales Engine[SM], which transitions into the mechanics of sales predictability. We began with the leadership mindset of The Culture of Commerce[SM] because it creates an atmosphere for interacting with customers; without it, selling efforts stall. My hope is The Culture of Commerce[SM] motivates leaders to consider all of their resources and the potential impact of adoption. The ROI and productivity gains are massive based on reduced customer turnover, increased wallet share from existing customers and the ability to attract new customers. Directing 100% of enterprise resources — people, process and technology — in a customer-centric fashion is powerful because it creates disciples, and ultimately, growth.

THE SALES ENGINE^{SM}
The Roadmap to Sales Predictability

CHAPTER **3**

*"Unless you have a reliable, duplicatable, scalable and consistent way
to bring potential customers in, you don't have a business, you have a hobby."*
—*Mark Cuban, Businessman and Investor*

N ow that you're sold on The Culture of Commerce^{SM} as a leadership mindset, we need to address the sales model. Let's be real. A company is hard-pressed to lay claim to The Culture of Commerce^{SM} without having a sales model that produces a continuous flow of new opportunities resulting in new customer relationships. I call this road map to sales predictability "The Sales Engine^{SM}."

Why is The Sales Engine^{SM} relevant?

I've found most sales teams to be mediocre, with a few top producers and then everyone else, resulting in enormous performance gaps among sales reps and inconsistent sales results for enterprises. For organizations struggling with this reality, there are only a few explanations:

- One, they're deploying an outdated sales model.
- Two, they've got the wrong people on their sales team.
- Three, they have an execution problem.

The Sales Engine^{SM} answers one and three by providing an irrefutable sales framework that can be implemented quickly and effectively. All that's required of the enterprise is to resource

33

The Sales Engine^{SM} with time, talent and capital. That's not to understate the challenge of time, talent and capital. However, implementing an irrefutable sales model and executing against it is far more achievable than rethinking one's sales model, execution and resourcing. If your company is grappling with inconsistent sales results and performance gaps between reps, read on!

The Sales Engine^{SM} is a business-agnostic framework applicable to solution-based, consultative and transactional B2B selling scenarios. My background is selling for B2B manufacturers, distributors, software consulting and service providers, all of whom rely on a variety of selling scenarios. Let's walk through each one so we're on the same page.

In the case of transactional sellers, the hardest worker wins. Transactional sellers can be identified by those selling mature products or services, available from a number of sources with very little differentiation among them. Transactional sellers call on buyers who make decisions based on price, quality and availability/delivery. For transactional sellers, winning business is a function of making as many sales calls as possible, knowing they'll close a portion of the real, active opportunities in their pipeline.

Solution-based sellers are solving an industry problem after fact-finding, identifying a failure mechanism or unacceptable outcome and introducing their solution to the customer. Like their transactional counterparts, solution-based sellers must cast their net wide and deep. They must also understand their sales approach won't resonate with all buyers, so their opportunities will be few and focused.

Consultative sellers engage in discovery with the customer, identify a business outcome that excites the buyer and then quantify the outcome to close the sale. Consultative sellers tend to focus on niche markets and, because their sales cycle is time-consuming for them and their prospects, opportunity pipelines are thin. Consultative sellers educate, offer unique business insights to their customers and engage in a thorough process to demonstrate capabilities and thought leadership while taking the time to understand their customer's business goals. Consultative sellers go to extreme measures to clearly articulate their feature set, implementation process and the team supporting the customer post-sale. Since their relationship with the customer is more like a marriage, how the consultative seller engages with the customer pre- and post-sale often dictates winning or losing the business. It's common for consultative sellers to agree on a proof of concept with the client that, once validated, justifies a larger investment downstream.

As you've likely picked up, consultative sellers are generally involved in large deal sizes with lengthy sales cycles. Solution-based sellers offer premium-based products or services sometimes involving a trial to validate their solution. Solution sellers are somewhere in between consultative and transactional sellers on deal size and length of the sales cycle. Transactional sellers have short sales cycles and smaller deal sizes, and most of their effort is spent trying to alter purchasing patterns to get their first sales opportunity. So, although the transactional sellers' process is far simpler than their solution-based and consultative counterparts, significant work is required to alter the prospect's purchasing patterns because, let's face it, humans are creatures of habit.

It's important to point out that each of the successful sellers in the three selling scenarios discussed here have a unique skill set. One is no more intelligent than the other — just different, based on the products and services they sell.

Let's get into the components that make up The Sales Engine^{SM}. Each will be expanded on in subsequent, dedicated chapters.

Compelling Message – All B2B companies need a message that rocks. Various forms of that message need to be available and tailored to different buyer personas to address their unique considerations and where they're at on the sales continuum. A weak message that doesn't resonate places undue pressure on the sales team and other components of The Sales Engine^{SM}.

Lead Generation – Lead generation is what fuels The Sales Engine^{SM}. Imagine having a high-performance sports car in the driveway on a sunny day. It's sitting there beckoning you to drive it. You grab the keys, get into the car and turn on the ignition. As you begin to drive, you remember that you filled up with low-octane fuel when, in fact, this particular engine thrives on high-octane fuel. Oh no! The car drives, but it clearly isn't performing the way you know it can. Like a high-performance sports car, The Sales Engine^{SM} requires the right kind of fuel. Similarly, many B2B companies spin their wheels by not wisely considering their best lead generation options for The Sales Engine^{SM}.

Digital Strategy – Today, all B2B enterprises are selling to a digital buyer. With this new reality comes an opportunity to both extend a company's reach and accelerate the buying journey for customers. This can be accomplished through digital strategy, which may comprise the company website, being found in the search engines through SEO and SEM and continuously evolving the strategy through data-driven decisions supported by analytics. You may find the term "digital strategy" overly broad, but my focus is exclusively on using technology to facilitate commerce. Specifically, identifying opportunities to increase the flow of commerce and ratchet up new customer acquisition by removing constraints and advancing the sales process online (digitally).

Defined Selling Process – The primary reason to follow a defined selling process is to manage customer conversations in a consistent manner. This doesn't mean sales teams win every deal, but it does ensure opportunities are run through a methodical process. Ultimately, customers want to be understood and educated and be able to share their expectations and needs so solutions can be placed within their context. Customers may resist this kind of process, but if that's the case, it's a red flag for sellers and likely a poor opportunity to pursue. Or perhaps it's indicative of a transactional selling scenario, meaning, "You sell it, I buy it — what's the price and delivery?" Sellers win deals and longtime relationships when the sales process is about improving the customer's condition or achieving a business outcome. The Sales Engine^{SM} has three sales zones that are both simple and effective: Sales Zone No. 1 is Education & Exploration; Sales Zone No. 2 is the Fit Zone; and Sales Zone No. 3 is the Decision-Making Zone. My belief is this defined selling process is applicable to most selling scenarios and relevant to the majority of B2B sales organizations.

Sales Toolbox – All sales teams need access to sales and marketing assets they can draw upon to advance the sales process. Examples of assets include demos, a company website, case studies, presentations, content, industry insights, customer success stories and more. Unique content assets allow the sales team to address different buyer personas throughout the selling process.

The Sales Team – The Sales Team provides selling capacity and a skill set. A major component of The Sales Engine^{SM} is generating sufficient cycles to reach growth goals. Without pure selling capacity, generally accomplished through deploying people in specific sales channels, it becomes challenging to generate enough cycles or opportunities to achieve sales targets. In addition to capacity, the sales team brings a unique skill set required to nurture opportunities along the sales continuum, manage and direct customer conversations and close deals. I have a friend who is one of the most charismatic sales leaders I've ever met, and she will tell you the most important characteristics of salespeople are attitude and activity. The sales team's skill set needs to go beyond attitude and activity, but I agree that these two attributes are the price of admission for salespeople. Attitude and activity are baseline; without them, success isn't achievable. Later, we'll discuss other skill sets required to unleash successful cycles and scale the business. *(See graphic on next page)*

The Sales Engine^{SM} is a cohesive sales and marketing strategy that produces consistent results. At the center of the infographic, you'll notice the sales continuum that runs from zero to 10, left to right. A high-performing sales engine will be flowing with high-quality opportunities through the sales continuum at all times. At zero, the prospect is barely familiar to your business. At 10, the opportunity has moved through the sales process to *deal* or *no deal*.

In the far left-hand side of the infographic, you'll notice The Sales Engine^{SM} is fueled with lead generation. The methods of lead generation outlined are certainly not exhaustive, but the most commonly used in the B2B marketplace. All methods of lead generation travel through the company website before the prospect lands somewhere on the sales continuum.

Because the website content is thoughtfully mapped to the buying journey, offering specific information to different buyer personas, the prospect is able to self-qualify in or out of the

The Sales Engine℠ – The Roadmap to Sales Predictability

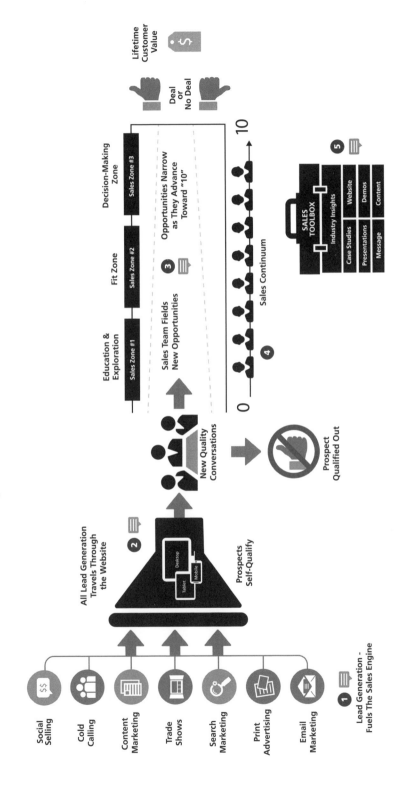

Legend: ⬚ Compelling Message ❶ Lead Gen ❷ Digital Strategy
❸ Defined Selling Process ❹ The Sales Team ❺ Sales Toolbox

THE**HALPIN**GROUP
©2019 The Halpin Group, LLC

buying process. That's right, people. The website acts as a sales accelerator — so productive that prospective buyers can conduct pre-purchase research autonomously without speaking to a salesperson (at least initially). In fact, today we know that the customer journey is 57% complete before a prospect's first contact with a potential supplier. Once a prospect self-qualifies into the selling process, they are dropped onto the sales continuum where they can submit an inquiry and connect with a salesperson to discuss their specific need. When a first interaction takes place between a buyer and seller will differ depending on selling scenarios. You'll notice three distinct sales zones above the sales continuum.

- Sales Zone No. 1 – Education & Exploration Zone
- Sales Zone No. 2 – Fit Zone
- Sales Zone No. 3 – Decision-Making Zone

Depending on the method of lead generation, a prospect could begin at zero on the sales continuum or somewhere further along. I'd suggest that the more compelling the content used with lead generation and on the website, the more likely they'll get further along the sales continuum or, from their side, the buying journey. As a reference point, I'd suggest referrals begin at six or seven on the sales continuum, meaning salespeople can bypass Sales Zone No. 1 and begin at the end of Sales Zone No. 2. This is because referrals provide trust and credibility, accelerating the sales or buying process, depending on which side of the table you sit.

Sales Zone No. 1

In Sales Zone No. 1, the conversation is simply education and exploration, which equates to a meaningful two-way discussion where the salesperson learns the basics of the prospect's business, and the prospect gets a sense of the seller's products and services, the types of customers they serve and the business outcomes they typically deliver. The seller should uncover the buyer's immediate need or the problem they're trying to solve, but also expand the conversation at the appropriate time. In Sales Zone No. 1, which could be one or several conversations, both parties decide if it makes sense to move into the next step. The best way to end every customer conversation is, "Where do we go from here?" or "What's the next step?" To have meetings that don't end with either of those questions is inexcusable, because time is money. The answer indicates each party's level of interest, if it makes sense to continue the conversation and outlines specific action items to make the next meeting productive. The following are examples of my go-to questions in a Sales Zone No. 1 meeting:

- Describe to me your typical customer? "We have three customer types: production machine shops, job shops and distributors."
- Do you have a preference on which you sell to? "I'd prefer to not sell through distributors

and sell direct whenever possible." Why? "I want a one-to-one relationship with the end user so we can build our brand and not battle for mindshare with the distributor. The web allows me that opportunity, and I want to take full advantage."

- What is your average deal size in dollars? "$900."
- What about product mix? Is there a product mix that's more profitable than others? "We have three different product groups: standard catalog cutting tools, custom cutting tools and re-grinding/resharpening services. Margins differ slightly among the three, but not enough to pursue one more aggressively than another." Would you like to see one of the three outgrow the others? I ask because I'm wondering if there is a margin benefit or competitive advantage your company brings in one area over another. "Actually, we like to see balance in all three areas with one exception. We would like to have more customers taking advantage of our resharpening/regrinding services because we have unlimited capacity and it makes the relationship sticky — it helps us stay in front of them in between orders for new tooling."
- How do you go to market? "We use independent reps and have 12 in total. I'd say about four of the independent reps generate 80% of our sales, and the balance is less active. We also have approximately 100 house accounts that we manage internally."
- Do you see strategic opportunities for growth, and if so, can you share a few of them? "Sure. We have three focus areas. First, we plan to invest aggressively in digital marketing to capture and convert customers online. We've been slow to react to the emerging digital buyer, but that's going to change with a new website, product search and selection tools and search marketing services. Second, we're continuously reviewing new machining technology to find operational productivity and efficiencies in the shop. When we find the right machining centers, we invest. Third, we have to attract new talent to our workforce."

As you can see, I've just uncovered incredible information that allows me, as the seller, to position my products, services and solutions in the customer's context. I'm now able to have a high-impact conversation in Sales Zone No. 1.

Sales Zone No. 2

If the conversation moves to Sales Zone No. 2, it indicates the education and exploration conversations went well and it's appropriate to transition to the customer's immediate need, requirement or problem they're looking to solve. For example, if selling software, Sales Zone No. 2 would be made up of scoping discussions where the solution is outlined and the output is a statement of work or requirements document so all parties are clear on the ultimate deliverable. Sales Zone No. 2 may also be the time to discuss a pilot or trial. If selling a solution, you might spend time understanding the customer's failure mechanism in order to steer them into the correct solution. If it's a transactional sale, Sales Zone No. 2 might involve understanding the customer's total spend in a given commodity and service level requirements so the seller can build the best commercial proposal possible to win the business.

On the customer side of Sales Zone No. 2, they're kicking the tires by seeking to understand the potential fit of the vendor. They're asking questions like:

- Describe your typical customer.
- Walk me through your core business.
- Are you willing to provide references so I can talk to a few of them?
- What business outcomes have you been able to provide to customers?
- How would our business stack up with other current customers?
- Tell me about your post-sale support process.
- Can you explain the team structure supporting us throughout the project?
- What are your service levels?
- When you've encountered difficult projects, what have been the contributing factors?
- What's the return on investment of your solution?
- Do you have relevant case studies you can share with me?
- Can I meet the team that will be supporting us post-sale?

In Sales Zone No. 2, Fit Zone, the customer wants to ensure they don't enter into a bad marriage. Why? Because the cost of selecting the wrong vendor is too high. Conversely, the seller should have similar concerns, because a bad fit drains company resources and results in short-lived customer relationships. Both parties need to check the boxes, look for red flags and be open and honest about concerns in Sales Zone No. 2.

If both parties are satisfied with the conversations in Sales Zone No. 2, then it's generally agreed that statements of work, quotes, proposals, agreements or contracts need to be created for consideration in Sales Zone No. 3. However, if both parties aren't satisfied with the conversations in Sales Zone No. 2, then generally one or both parties opt out of the conversation based on poor fit — which, by the way, is totally okay.

Too often I find sellers thinking every customer is a good fit. That's a dangerous mindset because it results in toxic relationships. I've seen bad fits resulting from cultural differences, miscommunication, expectation gaps and disparate operating models. It can be painful. Upon accepting that an existing client is a bad fit, I have a friend who will tell the client, "Hey, let's not do this anymore. This isn't working. Let's schedule a meeting to discuss a transition process so we can support your team finding another vendor that's a better fit." What a great approach to a bad situation! However, if the seller had noticed red flags during the sales process, the customer could have been qualified-out early on. Of course, that's the incongruency between hitting sales goals and selecting the right customers. Salespeople want to achieve or surpass their numbers, which can result in onboarding clients who should have never been sold. This is the tension we live in as sales pros.

The perfect scenario in Sales Zone No. 2 is when the buyer and seller have entered into a trial or pilot and validated their solution with quantifiable results. This enables the seller to build a business case for a larger investment and gain a sense of what it's like to work together.

On the other hand, if it's obvious to both parties there is a fit and the buyer is interested in a timely transformative change, a trial or pilot may not be necessary. It all depends upon the complexity of the deal, the nuances of the selling/buying scenario and the desired pace of change.

The longer the conversation continues into Sales Zone No. 2, the more likely the opportunity is moving toward a decision, or Sales Zone No. 3.

Sales Zone No. 3

In Sales Zone No. 3, The Decision-Making Zone, it's time to advance the conversation to deal or no deal. A salesperson can be confident they're entering Sales Zone No. 3 when:

- It's clear to both the buyer and seller that their companies are a fit.
- The buyer's questions and objections have been thoroughly and satisfactorily addressed.
- The seller has clearly differentiated their unique selling proposition and made a compelling case that they should be the supplier or service provider of choice.
- The customer has communicated a timeline in which they intend to make a decision.
- The conversation is active and the customer has demonstrated the will to take action and bring the conversation to a close.
- Lots of questions are being asked about post-sale support, service levels or the implementation process.

Sales Zone No. 3 is incredibly important. At this point in the process, the buyer is mostly satisfied with what they've learned throughout and the conversation is ready to advance toward a decision. The seller has successfully communicated the company's credibility, authority and leadership or has run point in a team-selling scenario typical of enterprise or major account sales. In Sales Zone No. 3, the elements of the agreement are documented with commercial terms and conditions, timelines and details of the deliverable. Agreements serve as documentation of the deliverable for both the buyer and seller. Deal structure is simple in transactional selling scenarios and more challenging in complex consultative and solution-based selling scenarios.

I've found the key to closing a high percentage of opportunities is having a coach in the buyer's organization to provide candid, honest feedback to help the seller close the deal — essentially, a person who says, "If you edit this and commit to that, we can execute the agreement." Or, "Our major concern is X. If you can help address that concern, we'll award you the work." Without someone coaching the seller, it becomes hard to bring the sales process to a close.

When opportunities move into Sales Zone No. 3, I find myself spending a lot of time discussing how the customer will be supported post-sale. This indicates the customer wants to move forward with my firm because they're highly focused on the post-sale process, a potential transition from one vendor to another and often a successful implementation. High-performing salespeople can quickly pivot from the talking points of the deal to the actual implementation of the relationship. It's easier to make that pivot when the seller has complete confidence in their team to fulfill the promises made throughout the sales process — their team has adopted The Culture of Commerce^{SM}. I've learned that the ability to clearly articulate the post-sale transition is key to getting the customer to execute a proposal or agreement and bring the conversation to a close.

The three sales zones — the defined selling processes — are foundational to The Sales Engine^{SM} and, in upcoming chapters, we'll discuss best practices for managing customer conversations through each sales zone by explaining:

- How to Rock Your Message
- Directed Conversations & Active Listening
- The Sales Toolbox

Additionally, I'll explain the other elements of The Sales Engine^{SM} in detail, including:

- Lead Generation
- Digital Strategy
- The Sales Team

The goal is for readers to walk away with a clear understanding of The Sales Engine^{SM} and begin to implement it in their organization.

ROCK YOUR MESSAGE
Like a Good Melody, a Strong Message
Always Leaves a Mark

CHAPTER 4

"Information is giving out and communication is getting through."
—*Sydney J. Harris, U.S. Journalist*

For me, the ability to influence others is rooted in strong communication and messaging skills. Every other skill is a distant second. Similarly, for salespeople it's important to remember that thoughtful messaging separates high performers from the rest of the crowd. In reviewing The Sales Engine[SM] infographic, you'll notice the message icon appears in lead generation, digital strategy, throughout the selling process and even in the sales toolbox. That's not an accident. Top-producing salespeople know how, where and when to incorporate their message into the sales process for maximum impact.

Strong messaging is essential for sales teams to secure meetings, stand out from the competition and advance conversations with prospects. A well-crafted message is very much like a good melody. It stays with you. Although your message may not have the same emotional connection as a song, a succinct message is unique and leaves a lasting impression. *(See graphics on next two pages)*

The Rock Your Message Framework is intended to launch clients into a team-based content-building process focused on the essential points of your message. The output is rich content that can be structured, ordered and refined based on its intended use. For example, if the content is pitch material for the sales team, company website, general marketing collateral or

The Best Melodies Leave A Mark - So Should Your Message

THE BEST WAY TO ROCK YOUR MESSAGE

FOCUS

★ Business Outcome Your Solutions Provide

★ Industry Problem You Solve

★ Common Results Your Customers Typically Experience

★ Your Core Competencies

★ Your Core Customer

★ Authority & Leadership You're Known For Providing

Structure, Order & Refine Content Based Upon Intended Use

Messaging Framework - Compelling Language Secures Meetings, Advances Conversations & Differentiates

THE**HALPIN**GROUP

Positioning - Stand Out From The Crowd During The Sales Process

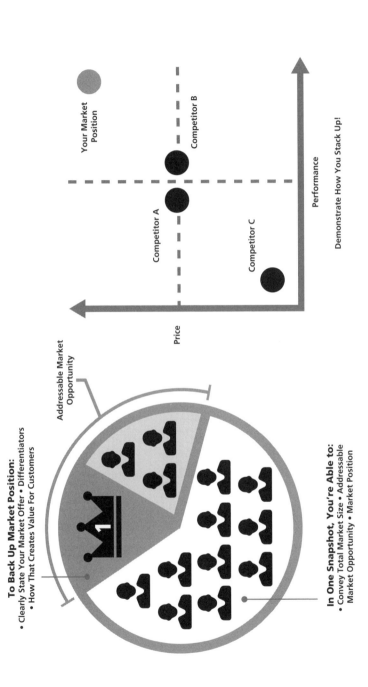

To Back Up Market Position:
• Clearly State Your Market Offer • Differentiators
• How That Creates Value For Customers

Addressable Market Opportunity

Your Market Position

Competitor A

Competitor B

Competitor C

Price

Performance

Demonstrate How You Stack Up!

In One Snapshot, You're Able to:
• Convey Total Market Size • Addressable Market Opportunity • Market Position

- Visual Tools Create More Meaningful Customer Conversations
- Inability to Position Indicates A Lack of Strategy

THE**HALPIN**GROUP
©2019 The Halpin Group, LLC

slide decks, it makes sense to use the content differently, in expanded or abbreviated formats, at different times in the sales process or customer journey. In The Sales Engine℠ framework, the message is needed throughout the sales process.

At the end of each element that follows, you'll notice an example that relates to the messaging for my consulting business.

The Rock Your Message Framework works like this:

Business Outcome Your Solutions Provide – Prospects, initially, are far more interested in business outcomes than solutions provided to them. Sales teams that message business outcomes get meetings. Period. As you get further into the sales process, drilling down into solutions becomes more natural for both the buyer and seller. Too many sales teams message products, services, processes and features without messaging benefits and business outcomes. At some point, it's necessary to talk about your solutions, but getting them out of order is a big mistake!
Example: "I help B2B companies grow their sales predictably."

Industry Problem You Solve – This is the bridge that connects the business outcome to your solutions while communicating your knowledge and insights into the prospect's world. To the buyer, it says, "You understand me."
Example: Many B2B companies suffer from sales mediocrity. They don't have a process for sales and, as a result, they experience inconsistent results. To make matters worse, their culture creates an unattractive atmosphere in which to do business. The result is a friction-filled customer experience. I introduce clients to The Sales Engine℠, an irrefutable, business-agnostic framework that supports all selling scenarios and creates sales predictability. But that's not enough, because a predictable sales framework is meaningless without a strong company culture to support it. To help my clients achieve a transformation in culture, I teach clients about The Customer Prevention Culture℠ and its remedy, The Culture of Commerce℠. The result is a standard and framework to deliver frictionless customer experience.

Common Results Your Customers Typically Experience – The goal is to communicate, "Clients that hire us experience x, y and z within three months of implementation." This is the opportunity to make bold, fact-based, quantifiable statements with timelines.
Example: Clients who hire me typically experience the following within 12 months of engagement:
  1. The implementation of a robust sales engine.
  2. An enhanced digital strategy to drive lead gen, sales acceleration and productivity.

3. *A strong message for the sales team to take into the marketplace.*

4. *A complete sales toolbox inclusive of demos, presentations, industry insights and case studies.*

5. *Increasingly consistent results among territories and reps.*

6. *Visibility of cultural misalignment and the impact to customer experience.*

Note: Common results can be translated to quantifiable statements based upon certain assumptions and the target audience.

Your Core Competencies – Identify the unique or specialized knowledge within the organization that enables the development of products, services, intellectual property or whatever creates value for customers.

Example: "I'm an expert in simple and complex B2B selling scenarios. My teams have represented more than 40 businesses over the past 15 years, having successfully sold products and services, including steel, software, digital marketing solutions and consulting services. My core competencies include sales strategy, messaging, sales execution, sales channels, transactional selling, solution selling, major/enterprise account sales, digital marketing and sales leadership. These competencies are supported by introducing unique business-agnostic frameworks to help clients transform their sales trajectory and culture."

Your Core Customer – Clearly communicate the types of customers you're interested in pursuing. What's conveyed here is that you understand the target market, the learning curve is short and you're a known and trusted resource. Why? Customers place value on vendors they don't have to pay to learn on the job.

Example: "I work with B2B manufacturing, distribution and service providers. My network of relationships spans 20 years, and my goal is to impact a client's selling process favorably and sustainably."

Authority & Leadership – If your company hasn't found its authority, I highly recommend investing the time to identify it. It's one thing to have subject matter expertise, but it's another to be known for having subject matter expertise (i.e., thought leadership). A question to ask of your team is, "What are we best at? If we claim authority or leadership in a specific discipline, does the market view us similarly and do we have evidence to back it up?" The end game is to message your authority and leadership in the market served and back it up with credible statements. When messaged properly, the company is clearly positioned in the context of your competition and target market.

Example: "My teams have sold more than $150 million in a variety of complex B2B selling scenarios. I've been hired to turn around underperforming business units, collaborate on sales and mar-

keting strategy, establish new sales channels and help clients design and build digital strategy. Few can offer the sales experience I bring to client engagements; my frameworks educate and influence sales teams to become more effective sellers and unify the entire company through alignment and shared organizational outcomes."

Let me share an example of how the output of the Rock Your Message framework might be used to in an abbreviated format.

Most salespeople, especially those focused on pursuing new business, will tell you their biggest challenge in life is getting first meetings with prospects.

The following is a three-part formula I call "Break Down The Door" and it's made up of Effort, Message and Tactic (EMT).

All three parts are interdependent, which means you must do all three well in order to get results.

Effort: Comes down to getting enough touches with prospects through phone calls, introductory emails or social selling. Effort is 100 percent controllable by the salesperson. If a salesperson believes in what they're selling and has a track record of positively impacting their customers' businesses, they'll likely put forth the effort. Effort is about hunger, being money-motivated and many other underlying factors that cause producers to work hard.

Message: Most prospects don't care about your product or service, but they do care about the business outcome your product or service provides. Therefore, it's important that you translate your product or service to a business outcome and message your common results, which were elements we covered in Rock Your Message. Here is my message for first calls with prospects:

"My name is Tom Halpin and I help B2B clients transform their businesses by introducing new leadership mindsets, frameworks and implementation strategies." (WHO ARE YOU? WHAT IS YOUR CORE BUSINESS?)

"Many companies struggle with sales mediocrity and The Customer Prevention Culture^{SM}, where companies unintentionally introduce friction throughout the customer lifecycle. I help remedy the situation by introducing clients to The Sales Engine^{SM}, the roadmap to sales predictability and The Culture of Commerce^{SM}, a framework to build culture, drive sales and create disciples." (WHY SHOULD THE PROSPECT TALK TO YOU? WHAT INDUSTRY PROBLEM DO YOU SOLVE?)

Message your business outcome and common results:

"Clients who hire me typically gain the following within six to 12 months, depending upon the pace of the engagement:

"A process to generate predictable sales results.

"A strong message to take into the marketplace.

"A complete sales toolbox to advance conversations for all buyer personas.

"An enhanced digital strategy to drive lead generation, productivity and sales acceleration.

"Company-wide visibility of friction and misalignment within the customer experience.

"Team adoption of shared organizational outcomes." (MESSAGE YOUR BUSINESS OUT-COME AND COMMON RESULTS)

"Since I have worked with over 50 B2B clients over the last 15 years as both an independent sales rep and consultant, my teams have closed more than $150 million in sales. My experience in selling products and services both direct to the end user and through channel partners uniquely qualifies me to consult in simple and complex selling scenarios and, more importantly, shorten the learning curve." (SMATTER IN CREDIBILITY)

"Does it make sense for us to schedule an exploratory conversation next week?" (ASK FOR THE MEETING)

Tactic: The goal is to get a first meeting — nothing more. Avoid the common mistake of feature dumping, where you take all of your knowledge and unload it onto the prospect during an initial conversation. This is something I did early on in my sales career, and many salespeople fall into the same trap today. It's entirely inappropriate when your goal is to get a first meeting.

The key? Be succinct in how you fashion emails and phone calls, which boils down to structure and brevity. Salespeople need to be mindful of when to be brief and when it's more appropriate to have expansive conversations. Many salespeople don't have this skill, which can limit their results.

This example can be applied to phone calls, introductory emails and, on some level, social selling.

When EMT is put into practice, salespeople will book first meetings at a higher rate and be able to talk to a higher-level audience. They'll be able to call into the C Suite and talk to owners and other top decision-makers.

To recap, Rock Your Message is intended to prompt a creative content-building process. The process will likely require several edits before the message is distinctive and something the team can be proud of. Once done, you'll have strong, customer-centric content that can be used in different formats across a variety of media.

Strong messaging is enormously important to secure meetings, stand out from the competition and advance conversations with prospects. You'll know the sales team is Rocking Your Message when prospects and customers begin to repeat it. Why? Because compelling language always leaves a mark.

LEAD GENERATION
The Sales Engine Requires Fuel

"You're out of business if you don't have a prospect."
—*Zig Ziglar, American Author, Salesman and Motivational Speaker*

All engines need fuel, and lead generation is what fuels The Sales Engine[SM]. In the B2B world, conventional lead generation options include cold calling, print advertising, trade shows, content marketing, email marketing, search marketing and social selling. Reference The Sales Engine[SM] infographic to see that lead generation is where it all starts and, no matter which method of lead gen is employed, all leads come through the website where prospects self-qualify in or out of the sales process. Some may take issue with the suggestion that *all leads* come through the website. To that I say, even if it's not 100% true today, we all need to think this way because, at some point soon, 100% of our prospects will be digital consumers. To get the most out of lead generation, incoming leads must be fielded properly. Let's look at an example. *(See graphic on next page)*

Lead Gen Requires Good Fielding

A manufacturer hired a search marketing agency to drive lead generation. As part of the process, customer phone calls and website forms were monitored to measure lead quality. Part of the process was to ensure calls and forms were being fielded appropriately and responded to

Lead Generation Fuels The Sales Engine℠

Education & Exploration — Fit Zone — Decision Making Zone

Sales Zone #1 | Sales Zone #2 | Sales Zone #3

Sales Team Fields New Opportunities

Opportunities Narrow as They Advance Toward "10"

New Quality Conversations

Prospect Qualified Out

Deal or No Deal

Lifetime Customer Value

Sales Continuum
0 — 10

SALES TOOLBOX
Industry Insights
Case Studies | Website
Presentations | Demos
Message | Content

Social Selling | Cold Calling
Content Marketing | Trade Shows
Search Marketing | Print Advertising
Email Marketing

Lead Generation - Fuels The Sales Engine

Prospects Self-Qualify

All Lead Generation Travels Through the Website

Legend:
Compelling Message ❶ Lead Gen ❷ Digital Strategy
❸ Defined Selling Process ❹ The Sales Team ❺ Sales Toolbox

THE **HALPIN** GROUP
©2019 The Halpin Group, LLC

in a timely manner. The manufacturer used its estimating team to be the first line of customer contact to qualify opportunities and quote new jobs.

The manufacturer's business was focused on producing automotive stamping dies for OEMs and tier suppliers. A call came in from a Japanese OEM and the agency thought they'd hit the motherlode. To put the call in perspective, it was the kind of opportunity that doesn't grow on trees. As I listened to the recorded call, the Japanese OEM introduced himself and clearly explained his intent, which was to develop new tooling sources in the Midwestern U.S. From there he began asking very specific questions of the estimator about the manufacturer's capabilities. Unfortunately, the estimator wanted no part of the conversation, wouldn't engage with the caller at any depth and was trying to get off the phone. It was beyond awkward.

As a follow-up, the sales rep for the search marketing agency scheduled a face-to-face meeting with the business owner to discuss the call and get his reaction. The sales rep's hope was to direct the conversation toward sales training for the estimating team to support the lead generation program. To the sales rep's amazement, the owner wasn't bothered by how the call was handled and wasn't interested in pursuing opportunities regarding how his estimating team fielded customer inquiries. The owner felt the caller only wanted information and had no intention of building a relationship.

While it's possible this conversation was going nowhere, it's the wrong way to handle incoming leads. The best approach, at this stage, is to avoid making disqualifying statements and get the conversation further along before determining if there is a fit. This call was absolutely in Sales Zone No. 1, which is entirely about education and exploration. What does that mean? Simply put, to have a healthy two-way exchange of information to determine if it makes sense to take the next step. The estimator's objective should have been threefold: understand the customer's business goals and pain points; learn more about the OEM's supplier development process; and position his company by clearly articulating their unique selling proposition in the context of the larger marketplace. Then recap the conversation and, if it made sense, agree on next steps. What if he would have uncovered pain that his company was uniquely positioned to solve? He didn't allow for that opportunity to happen. Instead, he made the decision to shut down the conversation, which we later learned through the owner's response was a symptom of The Customer Prevention Culture[SM].

How to Consider Lead-Generation Options

My advice to anyone in the B2B marketplace would be, at minimum, to scale back trade shows immediately and preferably abandon them altogether. Trade shows, in my opinion, are an outdated institution and most companies participate out of fear and historical decision-making.

The fear is that competitors will speak ill of them or customers will assume something negative from their lack of participation. Historical decision-making goes back to, "We've always exhibited at Metalworking World, so we must continue to do so." Trade shows are incredibly expensive and highly challenging to measure return on investment. Therefore, I recommend redeploying resources into more efficient lead-gen alternatives.

Print advertising as a form of lead generation also needs to be reevaluated. For companies engaged in a comprehensive print advertising strategy and whose marketing budgets are limited, consider redeploying those resources elsewhere. Today's buyers, influencers and approvers are online, and print has limited reach. I will acknowledge print advertising can be an effective form of brand building when used strategically and in a measured fashion. However, I'm a firm believer in *opportunity cost, the value of the next best thing you give up whenever you make a decision.* As it relates to lead generation, although there can be inherent good in trade shows and print advertising for many companies, consider what's being given up as a result of those decisions — I suspect you'd be giving up some potential high-impact lead-generation opportunities.

High-Impact Lead Generation

For me, there are three lead-generation activities that all B2B marketers need to employ to effectively reach today's buyers. They include content marketing, social selling and search marketing.

Content Marketing: Content marketing is the price of admission in today's climate. *Content marketing is a strategic marketing approach focused on creating and distributing valuable, relevant and consistent content to attract and retain a clearly defined audience — and, ultimately, to drive profitable customer action.*[1] Content marketing takes time and effort, but when executed within an overarching theme, content can be displayed across different media and repurposed depending on the use case.

Consider all of the professional sports leagues. They produce video game highlights, which then become shareable or "viral." Now it's true that very few B2B companies have budgets comparable to professional sports leagues, but I offer this example because it represents the dream.

How can B2B companies create compelling shareable content? My best advice is to review the Rock Your Message framework. Additionally, it's wise to avoid delivering perpetual infomercials that fatigue your audience or portray your company as a nuisance. A good practice is to publish content that's both within your predefined themes and helpful to your target market. Let me be more specific: Publishing content doesn't always need to benefit you. It can and should be to benefit your audience and, by doing good, your business will benefit along the way. As an example, my

---

[1] *https://contentmarketinginstitute.com/what-is-content-marketing/*

consulting promise is, "I help industrial B2B companies grow their sales predictably." My themes for authoring, reposting and publishing content include relevant approaches and best practices in:

- Digital Strategy
- Content That Fits Around The Sales Engine^{SM} Ecosystem
- Strategy & Execution – Specific to Digital, Sales, Marketing and Customer Experience
- Leadership – Impactful Ideas and Frameworks That Multiply Influence or Create Outcomes
- Disruptive Trends in the B2B Marketplace and Strategies to Mitigate
- Content That Fits Around The Culture of Commerce^{SM} Ecosystem

All content must serve my core audience, which consists of industrial B2B distributors, manufacturers and professional service firms.

These themes and rules provide a filter to stay focused on what's important and position me as a resource with my audience. My goal is to brand myself as a thought leader in company culture, sales predictability, sales strategy and sales execution in the B2B marketplace. I want owners, influencers and sales leaders to think of me as the top trusted adviser for business outcomes. I want The Sales Engine^{SM}, The Culture of Commerce^{SM} and The Customer Prevention Culture^{SM} to become a part of everyday language in the B2B marketplace and for my name, content and consulting firm to be associated with it.

The big shift in today's selling environment is that buyers prefer to be educated rather than sold. B2B marketers need to take stock of this shift by integrating content marketing into both their lead gen and overall marketing strategy. *(See graphic on next page)*

Social Selling: For B2B marketers, the most relevant social media platform is LinkedIn. Social selling is simply engaging in content marketing and publishing it through social channels like LinkedIn, Instagram, Facebook and others.

There is a simple formula to leverage social selling.

1. Define your audience and build out your network (i.e., connect with them). As an example, if you sell inbound marketing, you may want to connect with people with the title of CMO, VP Marketing, Digital Marketing Manager, President, VP Sales, Call Center Manager, Customer Service Manager, Owner, etc.

2. Post valuable insights that your audience will find meaningful.

3. Post and connect consistently. If you post and connect inconsistently, social selling loses its impact and won't be effective.

4. Follow the rules and best practices outlined in content marketing so themes are established and you're not playing the perpetual infomercial.

The goal of social selling is to stay in front of your audience by providing relevant content so

Your Content Marketing Ecosystem

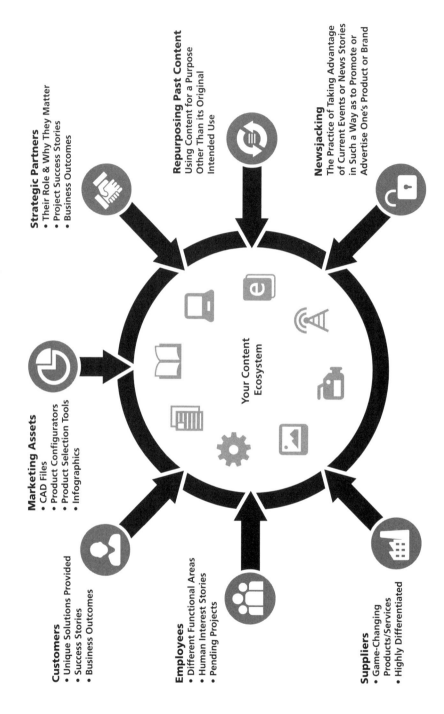

Strategic Partners
- Their Role & Why They Matter
- Project Success Stories
- Business Outcomes

Repurposing Past Content
Using Content for a Purpose
Other Than its Original
Intended Use

Newsjacking
The Practice of Taking Advantage
of Current Events or News Stories
in Such a Way as to Promote or
Advertise One's Product or Brand

Marketing Assets
- CAD Files
- Product Configurators
- Product Selection Tools
- Infographics

Customers
- Unique Solutions Provided
- Success Stories
- Business Outcomes

Employees
- Different Functional Areas
- Human Interest Stories
- Pending Projects

Suppliers
- Game-Changing
  Products/Services
- Highly Differentiated

Your Content
Ecosystem

Example - Content Sources & Mediums

THE**HALPIN**GROUP
©2019 The Halpin Group, LLC

you're seen as a thought leader in your areas of expertise. If the term "thought leader" is new to you, it's being known as a subject matter expert. The quality and consistency of posts will keep you top of mind within your network and position you for future conversations. LinkedIn is today's Rolodex, and because profiles are managed by the user, it helps everyone involved stay current with job and position changes and more.

I have a colleague who is highly active with social selling. After every new meeting with a prospect, he sends a LinkedIn connection request. His connections now exceed 2,000. He posts daily, and as a result, anyone who follows him is clear on his thought leadership. This allows him to create and grow relationships consistently. He is a sales leader for a full-service digital marketing agency whose client base largely consists of industrial distributors and manufacturers. The sales cycle he engages in generally requires multiple conversations before deals close. His social activity doesn't get him deals — it positions him for conversations that lead to deals. This is the outcome social selling provides.

LinkedIn published the following stats about social selling leaders[2]:

• Social selling leaders create 45% more opportunities than peers with lower SSI (Social Selling Index — see information that follows).

• Social selling leaders are 51% more likely to reach quota.

• 78% of social sellers outsell peers who don't use social media.

LinkedIn has established a Social Selling Index (SSI) that measures how effective you are at establishing your professional brand, finding the right people, engaging with insights and building relationships. It is updated daily. This is available only to subscribers of the LinkedIn Sales Navigator service.

Other social media channels may be relevant to your business. The key is understanding which audiences hang out on each platform and determining if connecting with each audience can be mutually beneficial. As an example, Instagram or Facebook may not provide B2B companies opportunities for lead generation, but could provide a platform for talent attraction. Keep these nuances between different social media platforms in mind.

Search Marketing: Search marketing is the process of gaining website traffic and visibility from search engines through both paid and unpaid efforts.

Search marketing encompasses:

SEO: Earning traffic through unpaid or free listings[3]

SEM: Buying traffic through paid search listings[4]

---

[2] https://business.linkedin.com/sales-solutions/social-selling/the-social-selling-index-ssi#

[3] https://searchengineland.com/guide/what-is-seo

[4] https://searchengineland.com/guide/what-is-paid-search

Originally called "search engine marketing," the shorter phrase "search marketing" is now often used as the umbrella term over SEO and SEM. The longer phrase "search engine marketing" — or SEM — is now typically used to describe paid search activities.[5]

Google is the largest sourcing guide on the planet, meaning buyers conduct their pre-purchase research in search engines and Google is the destination of choice. For companies serious about lead generation, investing in SEM and search engine optimization (SEO) heightens the probability of being found as prospective buyers are evaluating their sourcing options. Suppliers or service providers are found when the user clicks on a pay-per-click ad or organic listing and delivered into the company website after executing a keyword search in Google or Bing.

For some, this may be old news; others may feel their business is exempt from the emerging digital buyer. If you find yourself thinking search marketing doesn't apply to your business, I'd challenge you to make a modest investment in pay-per-click advertising (SEM), assuming your website is a professional representation of your business, articulates your value proposition and has a few simple calls to action. Install Google Analytics prior to launching the pay-per-click campaign and you'll quickly validate or disprove whether your target market uses Google for their sourcing needs.

Not only is SEM a great method for lead generation, but it also becomes a fantastic listening tool as advertisers gain visibility into the keyword queries entered into the Google, Yahoo or Bing search boxes. This is extremely important because most B2B companies use jargon in their respective trades that isn't necessarily aligned with how buyers think and search online. The actual SEM keyword queries act as listening tools and, when reviewed, allow your company to modify messaging and content in a customer-centric fashion by avoiding the pitfalls of static jargon.

The Story of Blueprint Manufacturing

I have a longtime client, Blueprint Manufacturing. They are a U.S.-based, family-owned manufacturer of custom cutting tools serving multiple industries including aerospace, hydraulics, automotive and defense. About six years ago, we met to discuss building a comprehensive digital strategy with measurable ROI. At the time, they had an outdated website that presented Blueprint poorly to the marketplace. After several meetings, we decided to work together by first building a website that included a searchable online catalog and then, post-launch, driving traffic to the site through SEM and SEO services. The ROI would be clearly measurable through analytics and other listening tools to evolve the digital strategy over time, but it was also necessary to improve the overall customer experience. In turn, Blueprint would share information such as website leads that resulted in both new quotes and new customers. Once the website launched,

---

[5] *https://searchengineland.com/guide/what-is-sem*

Blueprint experienced a 471% increase in website leads and booked enough new business to recover the cost of the website in four months.

Previously, Blueprint Manufacturing had gone to market through outside salespeople, independent reps and selling through distributors. This presented a tremendous opportunity to leverage a strong digital strategy to extend Blueprint's reach into the market, but in a cost-effective manner. Think about it. Prior to their digital strategy, developing new markets required hiring new salespeople, bringing on new independent reps and relying on distributors to sell their products. The digital strategy they've employed positions Blueprint Manufacturing to be found online by end users and yields lots of options. One, they can support incoming leads with their inside support staff. Two, Blueprint can refer the lead to their outside reps to mine the account for additional potential. Three, if Blueprint opts to refer the lead to a distributor, it provides incredible goodwill that hopefully leads to increased mindshare within the distributor's sales team. All options are winners.

Now that Blueprint has validated its first significant digital investment, the company can build on it with confidence that it will achieve a business outcome, whether focused on lead generation, sales acceleration or productivity.

Search marketing will undoubtedly evolve over time, and it's possible Google could fall out of favor or become less dominant. But that's not really the point. The point is, B2B companies need to understand where their target market hangs out online and be there! Doing so guarantees the investment into SEM and SEO will yield large returns by pairing intelligent lead generation with a thoughtful digital strategy.

In summary, content marketing, social selling and search marketing are musts for B2B marketers to drive high-impact lead generation, and they must be fully embraced to fuel The Sales Engine[SM].

DIGITAL STRATEGY
Capture and Convert Prospective
Buyers Online or Get Left Behind

CHAPTER **6**

"Be where the world is going." —Beth Comstock, American
Business Executive and Former Vice Chair, General Electric

Today, we hear the phrase *"digital transformation"* daily. Let's review a few definitions, because it's within this context that digital strategy takes shape.

"Digital transformation involves a change in leadership, different thinking, the encouragement of innovation and new business models, incorporating digitization of assets and an increased use of technology to improve the experience of your organization's employees, customers, suppliers, partners and stakeholders."[1]

"Digital Transformation (DX) is not necessarily about digital technology, but about the fact that technology, which is digital, allows people to solve their traditional problems. And they prefer this digital solution to the old solution."[2]

The topic of digital strategy is expansive and ever-changing, so I'm going to touch on a few important points and encourage readers to find trusted advisers to help navigate the landscape.

My perspective on digital strategy is simple: I believe in using digital technologies to grease the

---

[1] *http://www.theagileelephant.com/*

[2] *https://en.wikipedia.org/wiki/Digital_transformation*

skids of commerce and enhance organizational productivity. Specifically, I'm most interested in identifying opportunities to increase the flow of commerce and ratchet up new customer acquisition by removing constraints and advancing the sales process online. It's really important that companies seek out a digital agency or technology partner, or develop a competency in-house, because digital strategy is a key component of any cohesive sales and marketing strategy. A thoughtful and well-executed digital marketing strategy may be the most productive sales and marketing investment your company ever makes and can change the trajectory of your business. It's that big of a deal, so please don't miss the point.

In creating a digital strategy, I encourage companies to think in terms of three types of opportunities:

1. Lead Generation

2. Sales Acceleration

3. Productivity Tools

The three lead-generation tactics I recommend B2B companies pursue include content marketing, social selling and search marketing as outlined in the previous chapter. All three should be heavily skewed toward digital so that lead generation drives prospects to the company website where they can self-qualify in or out of the buying process.

Sales Acceleration

Many B2B companies go to market with one sales channel. As an example, let's say a business uses outside salespeople as their sole sales channel. This is the way they've sold since their inception and they don't see the need to change. The ability to scale their business using one sales channel is expensive and provides limited reach to customers. Assume a fully loaded cost of $150,000 per salesperson, inclusive of compensation, payroll tax, benefits, travel and more. Most companies would agree that the high cost of outside salespeople and their ability to be in front of a limited number of customers makes it an unsustainable model.

Furthering my point, we now know prospects prefer to conduct their pre-purchasing research online and that much of their buying journey is complete before their first conversation with a salesperson. This is the crux of why a thoughtful and well-executed digital strategy can have such tremendous impact to capture and convert prospects online and why it's a key component to The Sales Engine[SM]. After all, your digital strategy is working 24/7/365, and your salesperson is having only one conversation at a time. I'm a big fan of salespeople, but to deny the power of digital strategy is a major misstep. Let's consider a few supporting facts:

- 57% of the buying journey is complete before a prospect's first contact with a supplier.[3]

---

[3] *Source: Google/Millward Brown Digital, B2B Path to Purchase Study 2011, 2012 and 2014*

- 89% of B2B purchasers conduct their pre-purchase research online.[4]
- Google's mission "to organize the world's information and make it universally accessible and useful" has made it the largest sourcing guide on the planet.
- Search engines are efficient for both buyers and sellers — efficient for buyers because they can autonomously gather information and self-educate like never before, and efficient for sellers because they can reach buyers precisely as their pre-purchase research is happening (primarily through SEO and SEM).

Here are the key outcomes I believe B2B companies should have in mind when implementing a digital strategy:

- Attracting prospects by positioning their company website to be found in the search engines. How? Primarily through search engine marketing (SEM) and search engine optimization (SEO). Companies can either contract with an agency to manage SEM and SEO or hire digital marketing specialists in-house.
- The website needs to be a sales accelerator. A high-performing website converts visitors into leads. A conversion is any positive action a visitor takes, be it a phone call, form submission, PDF download, videos viewed and transactions in the case of an e-commerce business. How? By having clear calls to action on the website such as a prominently placed phone number, website forms and, of course, strong content. If a company sells via e-commerce, their product search, select and checkout experience should be on par with Amazon's. Many digital buyers bring B2C expectations into B2B e-commerce sites, and Amazon sets the standard.
- Keep the prospect in mind by mapping website content to the buyer's journey and, ultimately, offering up unique content to the different buyer personas the company serves. This action will help to make the website high performing and a sales accelerator. Buyer personas are semi-fictional representations of the types of people the company sells to regularly.
- Evolve and advance the digital strategy by using analytics and monitoring tools to make data-driven decisions. No digital strategy is set-and-forget or one-and-done. Reviewing analytics regularly allows the business to continuously improve the digital strategy based on what's being learned through online successes and failures.
- Use web applications to eliminate constraints in the organization and enable greater productivity. Stated another way: Identify friction within organizational workflows and determine if digital technology can unlock productivity and increase flow.

These examples are solid, tried-and-true opportunities for companies to pursue quick wins through digital investments. My experience is that opportunities for lead generation, sales accel-

---

[4] *Source: Google/Millward Brown Digital, B2B Path to Purchase Study 2011, 2012 and 2014*

eration and productivity exist in every organization. To get digital projects in motion, validating opportunities can be accomplished through proof of concepts or pilots — small projects that allow for modest investments to validate a strategy prior to going all-in with major investments. Pilots are validated or disproved by establishing success criteria to measure the change against baseline data (pre-implementation).

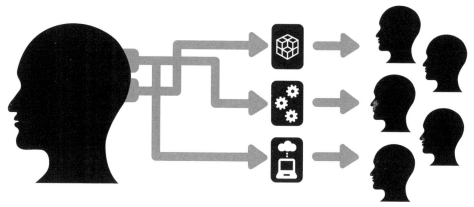

Example of Productivity Tools – Transfer Tribal Knowledge to Enable Productivity

Although I most often think about capturing and converting buyers online, there are other opportunities to employ digital strategy through productivity tools: for example, reviewing internal and external workflows by integrating technology to achieve a business outcome.

Across the board, I've found that most B2B companies have finite technical knowledge residing with an individual or subgroup. These specialists are valuable to the organization, but the isolation of their knowledge can also be a constraint to commerce, productivity and the development of other team members. Specialists may be well-intentioned people and freely give their knowledge away or, in some cases, hoard their knowledge as job security. Fortunately, there are solutions to transfer tribal knowledge to key stakeholders so team members, customers and organizations no longer have to be constrained by specialized knowledge residing with too few people.

Two enablers for transferring tribal knowledge are custom web applications and configurators. In both scenarios, the idea is to take product or manufacturing logic and build a web application or configurator to produce something of value, whether a smart part number, assembly or product configuration, 3D CAD model, price, technical drawing, bill of materials (BOM) or process routing (as examples). The web application or configurator is made up of inputs or a user interface (UI), logic and outputs. The outputs are highly customizable based on the client's business requirements. Inputs should be simple enough to be sales- and customer-facing.

During my interactions with industrial B2B clients, it's common to see organizational constraints in the following areas:

- Estimating & Quoting
- Technical Product Selection
- Product Configuration
- Custom Product Design & Build
- Engineering Constraints – Repetitive tasks and requests made by internal or external customers
- The Sales Queue – Any constraint slowing down customer opportunities or the selling process

The key takeaway is that configurator technology and web applications give organizations the ability to institutionalize specialized knowledge, making it accessible to the customers, channel partners and team members who need it most. The result is greater organizational productivity and commerce through knowledge transfer and accessibility.

Consider the business outcomes available to companies everywhere once they acknowledge the constraints holding their organizations back and inhibiting commerce. Think through how a configurator or web application could add value to customer engagement, operations or selling efforts. The ROI is likely to be within months and not years.

Blueprint Manufacturing, Continued

Earlier I shared a story about Blueprint Manufacturing and how they've successfully built a digital strategy that's yielding 10-15 new customers per month. With this success story under their belt, they want to discuss building a web application to eliminate a constraint in their estimating department. Currently their majority owner, Sam, quotes most of their work. His 40 years of experience, intimate knowledge of their operation and highly specialized experience in cutting tool design and applications make him uniquely qualified to quote most of their jobs. Estimating is important because if you get it wrong, the company loses money. Additionally, if pricing isn't competitive, you don't win business. Sam has tribal knowledge and, while it's awesome, if it doesn't get institutionalized, it becomes a constraint to commerce. Blueprint Manufacturing's estimating workflow hinges upon him touching most customer quotes; ultimately, his time would be better served recruiting talent, researching new machining technology and optimizing his company infrastructure to grow the business.

It would be naïve to think all tribal knowledge can be captured and automated. I'm not suggesting that at all. However, if 80% of Blueprint Manufacturing's estimating activity could be streamlined through a custom web application, we would have successfully increased the flow of commerce and freed up Sam to focus on more productive endeavors. Also, retirement is on the horizon for Sam, and he is in the process of building a succession plan. Part of that process will include him selling his shares in the business and, without a plan to transfer his tribal knowledge, the succession plan will stall. The solution we're discussing is a configurator that may be used internally or be customer-facing. It's too early to say. However, it will have a user interface (UI) with inputs, product logic and outputs. It will programmatically take the logic Sam currently uses manually to create an estimate and build it into a web application. We'll start by reviewing a subset of their overall business and build a proof of concept before expanding the web application to all products.

Where do constraints exist in your business? If the root cause is finite, technical knowledge residing in the heads of a few people, a productivity tool may be the answer. What is the outcome you envision? Specifically, what gets unleashed once the constraint is removed? What's the ROI to the business? I hope this gets your wheels turning! *(See graphic on next page)*

The Elephant in the Room – E-Commerce

At the time of this publication, B2B e-commerce in the U.S. is expected to exceed $1 trillion within two years and will continue to grow. The top 300 B2B e-commerce companies make up 64% of the total. It's a very exciting time, especially for those of us who work in the digital space. But if I had a dollar for every time I heard, "Salespeople will soon be obsolete as a result of e-commerce," I'd be a rich man. This is a sweeping oversimplification of what it takes to sell 100% of products and services and, more importantly, how customers want to engage with sellers. Are all companies dealing with a digital buyer today? Yes. Is it the price of admission to have a comprehensive digital strategy? For sure. Will some businesses sell exclusively through e-commerce? Yes.

However, the reality is e-commerce is best suited for very simple, transactional selling scenarios where the product has a SKU or part number, a simple set of attributes, a price and inventory status. Think in terms of low-consideration products and services — commodity items. When reloading on t-shirts, I'm not interested in engaging in multiple meetings, shopping the price and involving my colleagues in the decision-making process. E-commerce makes total sense in that buying scenario. And, of course, technology will enable more complex online transactions in the near future. However, generally speaking, more complex, higher-consideration products and services require educational and exploratory conversations and generally follow a process — these types of products are less conducive to e-commerce. Certainly the customer journey can be initiated and supported with a deliberate digital strategy. I believe that very much. But once a buyer self-qualifies into the buying process, a sales professional is often needed to nurture the opportunity.

Today, a big topic for large corporations is the idea of omni-channel marketing strategies. Omni-channel marketing is an acknowledgment that today's customer wants to engage through multiple channels on multiple devices. For example, customers may want to engage or transact online via mobile device, tablet or desktop. But they may also want access to a physical location, inbound customer service team, outside salesperson or e-commerce to support their buying needs. One feeds the other and supports growing the customer relationship. In some cases, companies choosing to implement an omni-channel strategy have the ability to sell exclusively through e-commerce. They simply ac-

Digital Sales Accelerators

1 Search

2 Website

3 Product Search & Selection Tools

4 Conversion

*Example Search

Google YAHOO! Bing

Pipe, Valves, Fittings

Sponsored Links

Organic Listings

User Clicks

Desktop

Tablet

Mobile

Online Catalog

CAD Files

Product Configurators

Transact

Phone Call

RFQ
Request for Quote

Download

Analytics

Industrial B2B Example

THE**HALPIN**GROUP

©2019 The Halpin Group, LLC

knowledge that customers want to engage in different ways depending on their needs.

So the next time a friend or colleague tells you salespeople are a dying institution, feel free to reframe the conversation, because it depends on a company's selling scenario and the needs of their target customer. In short, B2B companies need to educate themselves in order to employ the smartest digital strategy for their business and determine how and where e-commerce fits, if at all.

For those thinking through digital strategy, don't be intimidated. Often, non-technical business leaders play key roles in determining how technology can solve productivity breakdowns and frictional commerce. Use technology partners to vet solutions and vendors to select the best fit for the challenges facing your company. Frequently, the best digital strategies have more to do with digitizing business strategy than understanding technology.

As the digital strategy scales, additional tools will be needed, but they shouldn't prohibit companies from getting projects in motion early. For example, other needs will surface depending on the size and complexity of each business and where they are on their digital roadmap. Some considerations include:

• CRM (Customer Relationship Management) Software – The CRM houses contacts, contact history, sales pipeline information and more. Having a CRM is something all companies need because the alternative is having information stored in disparate systems or nowhere at all.

• Marketing Automation Software – Enables companies to automate basic tasks such as sequenced email campaigns targeted at prospects or customers who have opted-in to receive content from your company.

• Product Information Management (PIM) – A PIM is generally needed if a company sells through e-commerce or publishes to print and digital media, such as direct mail, print catalog, online catalog and more. A PIM is where all product information is mastered. Think of a PIM as the single source of truth for product information. It houses product images, product attribute data and other related information that can be published to multiple mediums (print or digital).

These are a few considerations for those committed to implementing a digital strategy. The CRM is a must-have, or your team will be handcuffed by not having one system of record and will instead be forced to manage spreadsheets. This is not a best practice.

In the end, all digital strategy should drive lead generation, sales acceleration and productivity. These three opportunities demonstrate why having a digital strategy is a key component of The Sales Engine[SM]. Additionally, examining how technology can be leveraged to institutionalize tribal knowledge can unlock enormous productivity in your organization. Using a digital strategy to help buyers self-qualify into the sales process is a powerful use of resources because, unlike humans, the website and related tools are not limited by time and space. This allows limited, high-value human capital to be deployed intelligently once prospects are far enough into the buying journey when human involvement becomes necessary to manage the conversation.

A DEFINED SELLING PROCESS
& THE SALES TOOLBOX
Managing Customer Conversations

CHAPTER 7

"The art of conversation lies in listening."
—Malcolm Forbes, Entrepreneur and Publisher

aving a defined selling process for the sales team helps to produce consistent, high-quality customer conversations. I recommend using a three-part defined selling process at all times:

- A Defined Process
    - o Sales Zone No. 1 – Education & Exploration
    - o Sales Zone No. 2 – Fit Zone
    - o Sales Zone No. 3 – Decision-Making Zone
- The Sales Toolbox to Advance Conversations
- Directed Conversations and Active Listening

Earlier we discussed the defined sales process comprised of Sales Zone Nos.1, 2 and 3. I believe in keeping things simple because we tend to overthink sales at times. Sales is all about having high-quality conversations and enough of them to ensure a predictable percentage actually close. A defined selling process is a means to that end. Period.

You might be thinking, *"What about creating PowerPoint decks for each scheduled meeting?"* Good question. If you commit to following my frameworks in Rock Your Message and Content Marketing, the Sales Toolbox will be full of assets that can be used repeatedly. I'll concede there may be some customization required based on what's learned in Sales Zone No. 1, but that should be very limited. It's far more productive for sales teams to be focused on building meeting agendas to prepare for dynamic customer meetings, rather than creating slide decks for every meeting. Since we discussed the sales zones earlier, let's jump into the other two parts of the three-part sales process.

The Sales Toolbox to Advance Conversations

I think of The Sales Toolbox as the central repository of sales and marketing assets I can pull from to move conversations along the sale continuum. As you recall, the sales continuum runs from zero to 10 and is broken down into Sales Zones Nos. 1, 2 and 3. The asset I decide to use depends on the questions and objections I hear from prospects, where we're at in the sales process and the type of customer in play. The more relevant the asset available in The Sales Toolbox, the more likely it is to advance the conversation in the sales process. The Sales Toolbox may include the following assets:

- Data-backed Industry Insights
- Demos
- PowerPoint Decks
- Website
- Multipurpose Content
  o Videos, whitepapers, blog posts, customer success stories, quantifiable business outcomes de-livered, common results
- Compelling Message
- Case Studies with Before and After Commentaries

These tools become very powerful when placed in the hands of high-performing salespeople, as they're used to advance customer conversations to *deal* or *no deal*. Smart salespeople know exactly where they're at in Sales Zones Nos. 1, 2 or 3, understand their prospect's objections and pull the most relevant assets from The Sales Toolbox for maximum impact. However, don't assume that all tools in The Sales Toolbox are sales and marketing collateral. Sometimes the best tools include skills and discipline.

Directed Conversations & Active Listening – Perhaps The Greatest Sales Tools Ever!

As a sales leader, my biggest pet peeve is salespeople who don't listen. Experience has shown me that many salespeople view customer meetings as an opportunity to "hold court." I find it obnoxious and rude. I've been known to kick colleagues under the table when I've noticed customers unsuccessfully trying to enter the conversation, being interrupted or having their sentences finished. Of course, listening is most effective when a salesperson directs the conversation by asking good questions and allows the customer to share information in an uninterrupted manner. The only excuse to break into the customer's response is to ask clarifying questions to further uncover something the customer has shared, reinforcing that you're actively listening and interested in what the client has to say. You can't fake active listening, by the way. Think about it.

Directed Conversations: Here is an example of how I might start a meeting:
"Thank you for meeting with us today. I forwarded an agenda ahead of time that we agreed would make for a productive meeting. But before we begin, I have a few questions that will help our team direct today's conversation. I want to be sure we cover information that's meaningful and relevant to your business goals."

- Describe your business to me. For example, is there a particular way you break down your business?
- Can you highlight your value proposition or market offer for me?
- Can you describe your competitive advantage?
- Describe your typical customer.
- What selling channels do you use, and how do you measure the effectiveness of each?
- What is your typical deal size? If it varies by business segment, feel free to elaborate.
- How many new customers do you activate in a year?
- Are KPIs or dashboards used for sales and marketing and if so, are you willing to share that information?
- Can you describe organizational constraints holding back your ability to grow or capture opportunities in the marketplace?

*(Note: Going through all of these might be too much and some might be covered in a pre-meeting, but they get the customer talking and sharing valuable information.)

The point of getting customers to share information is to identify specific areas of interest to them so the seller can ignore topics of little value to the customer and instead focus on meaningful points.

Active Listening: Let's set the stage. The customer has agreed to a meeting during prime time business hours to have a conversation. When a salesperson asks the right questions and then stops talking, they have the opportunity to gain insights and identify pain points, gaps or emerging areas of interest within the customer's business. Capturing that information enables the salesperson to tailor or position their solution in a way that not only meets the customer's business requirements, but potentially makes the competition irrelevant. This newfound information might justify a higher price or fee. It's also possible the solution delivered to the client can be repurposed and sold elsewhere. But without listening, this fountain of information never has the opportunity to be shared. Why? Because the salesperson valued talking over active listening.

In *The 7 Habits of Highly Effective People*, Stephen Covey gave us Habit No. 5, which is "Seek First to Understand, Then to be Understood." Active listening is very similar.

The following are tips for salespeople interested in the practice of active listening.

Do not:

- Interrupt the customer mid-sentence.
- Talk over the customer.
- Be a story stealer.
- Finish the customer's sentences.
- Think of your response while the customer is answering your questions.
- Feature dump: "My product/service does this, this, this and these three other things. And wait, there's more!" Think of a massive run-on sentence filled with features.

Do:

- Take notes.
- Listen with the intent to understand.
- Ask clarifying questions to further understand a point. (Note: This should be done in a way that doesn't interrupt the flow of the conversation. Jot down notes and interject with questions when appropriate — this may be later in the meeting and requires finesse.)
- Recap important points at the end of the meeting to make sure you accurately understand the content and context of what was shared.
- End your meetings with, "What is the next step?" or "Where do we go from here?" and document each one.
- Agree on a timeline for follow-up and make it happen!

Within The Sales Toolbox, directed conversations and active listening might be the greatest tools available to sales professionals. If you begin to have directed conversations and become an active listener, you'll have productive customer meetings, advance more sales opportunities and close more business.

More importantly, customers will take note of your consultative nature, separating you from the pack. Why? Because rather than ramrodding your product, service or solution down the customer's throat, you've taken the time to understand their business, which provides an opportunity to create a meaningful business outcome with quantifiable results. During these productive conversations, sellers may even identify value-added services for a commoditized product or stumble onto a solution that creates unique customer value. Most importantly, sellers will be positioned to agree on meaningful success criteria, setting the stage for a mutually beneficial, long-term relationship.

THE SALES TEAM
That Would Be All of Us!

CHAPTER **8**

"To me, job titles don't matter. Everyone is in sales. It's the only way we stay in business."
—Harvey Mackay, Businessman, Author and Syndicated Columnist

For the purposes of this chapter, I want you to think of The Sales Team, capitalized, as the entire organization and the sales team (lowercase) as the traditional group responsible for selling new customers and managing existing customer relationships.

I've lost track of the number of times I've heard, "I'm not in sales!" from a colleague who didn't have the word "sales" in their title, to which I always reply, "Ah, yes you are!" The back and forth that follows makes for a fun conversation because it requires a paradigm shift to accept that we're all part of The Sales Team. If I'm honest, I enjoy the sport of pushing back and challenging. This particular argument or mindset — that we're all part of The Sales Team — requires a more comprehensive view of how our organizations deliver and support customer relationships. Further, it requires a broader view of the atmosphere in which we conduct business. If we isolate our focus to The Sales Engine℠ framework, many would argue The Sales Team should only consist of the group that interacts with the sales model and has unique responsibilities for prospecting, lead follow-up, nurturing opportunities through the sales continuum and onboarding new customers. *(See graphic on next page)*

After all, we all have specific roles and responsibilities in our day-to-day positions. However,

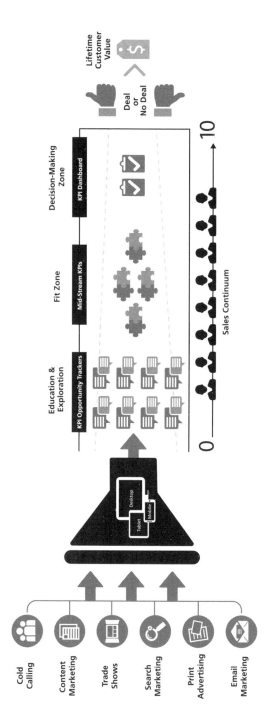

The Sales Engine
Growth Requires Generating Enough
New Quality Conversations & Advancing Them
Through The Sales Process

Making the Math Work in Your Favor

I would argue we also have common roles and responsibilities, and those who don't adopt this mindset likely suffer from The Customer Prevention Culture^{SM}. Salespeople in The Customer Prevention Culture^{SM} feel unsupported, as they likely spend a ton of time selling internally, insulating the customer from internal friction and taking the brunt of aligning and educating fellow team members to make sure customer deliverables are on-point. What a monumental waste of time! This is the primary reason I developed The Culture of Commerce^{SM} framework: to help B2B companies everywhere understand the core principles that shape frictionless commerce and customer experience. The Culture of Commerce^{SM} is a team mindset because adoption extends beyond the sales team.

Let's review the five principles of The Culture of Commerce^{SM} again.

1. The Customer is King!

2. Customer-Centric Infrastructure – People, Process and Technology

3. One Team – One Goal

4. All Customer Touchpoints Build or Break Confidence

5. Values Form Culture

To provide context, review The Customer Journey graphic one more time.

(See graphic on next page)

If we're honest, not only should it be acknowledged that the five principles supporting The Culture of Commerce^{SM} are far too big a burden for the sales team to bear, but it's also logical that the entire team should play a role in conquering commerce, regardless of their position. Providing a frictionless customer experience is too complex not to have team buy-in company wide. For example, take any one of the five principles in The Culture of Commerce^{SM} framework and tell me how they get implemented without every single team member's participation, adoption and ongoing commitment? It just won't happen.

If non-salespeople don't like to identify as salespeople, I'd use it as an opportunity to shift company culture and create teachable moments. Some might argue, "Well, maybe we all work in customer experience, customer service or customer care, but I'm not sure we all work in sales." To that I'd say, okay, fine, any of these options is an improvement and aligns the culture in a customer-centric way. If the alternative is no change, I'll take it. However, the big difference between these options and the entire organization becoming a part of The Sales Team is that salespeople are held accountable to a sales goal, their day-to-day actions affect the sales goal and their behavior reflects that accountability. There is a sense of urgency with these accountabilities. This may sound like semantics, but high-performing salespeople will tell you otherwise.

I'd also argue that strong salespeople are incredibly customer-centric because they have a

The Culture of Commerce℠ – Delivering a Frictionless Customer Experience

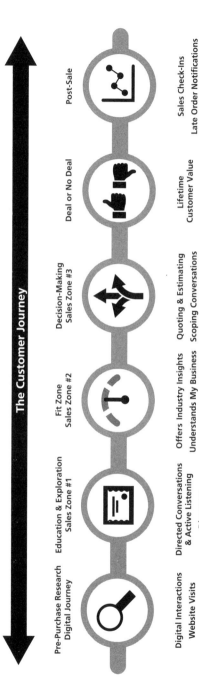

The Customer Journey

Pre-Purchase Research
Digital Journey

Digital Interactions
Website Visits
Digital Assets
Case Studies
Video
Downloads
Compelling Content
Mapped to Buying Journey

Education & Exploration
Sales Zone #1

Directed Conversations
& Active Listening
Discovery
Presentations
Not a Sales Call
But A Process

Fit Zone
Sales Zone #2

Offers Industry Insights
Understands My Business
Has Customers Like Me
Shows Capability
To Meet My Needs

Decision-Making
Sales Zone #3

Quoting & Estimating
Scoping Conversations
Negotiations
Project Plan
Implementation Plan
Tech Support

Deal or No Deal

Lifetime
Customer Value

Post-Sale

Sales Check-Ins
Late Order Notifications
Quote and Order Confirmations
Shipping Notifications
Price Increases
Change Orders/Addendum
Invoicing Inquires
Delivery Inquiries
Fulfillment
Part Identification
Ease of Use/Application

THE**HALPIN**GROUP
©2019 The Halpin Group, LLC

Points To Ponder: Customer Touchpoints Offer The Potential to Build or Break Confidence.
Friction is Bad & Flow is Good! How Does Your Company Rate?

front-row seat to the customer's perspective, changes in marketplace conditions and the factors contributing to friction in the customer experience. They also have the most skin in the game because their compensation shapes their mindset. This, too, is an important takeaway as leaders consider how to marry compensation with team behavior to advance the organizational mission.

At the root of The Customer Prevention Culture[SM] is the lack of visibility and framework to show team members the interdependencies of their functional areas and the interconnectedness of their workflows. Initiating the entire organization into The Sales Team supports The Culture of Commerce[SM] through the principle of One Team – One Goal.

While the sales team has a distinct skill set to onboard new customers, I believe both sales results and customer experience would change for the better if every team member understood they, too, were responsible for sales. Every team member has a customer upstream or downstream of them. Whether the customer is internal or external is irrelevant, because all inputs and outputs ultimately affect the final customer. If you find The Culture of Commerce[SM] compelling, consider how to engage your collective talent in new and different ways. Truth be told, few people get it, which is why The Customer Prevention Culture[SM] is so pervasive. My argument is that serving customers, solving problems and building confidence in every customer touchpoint can't rest on the shoulders of a few, but fall instead on every team member in the organization!

This brings us full circle to the five foundational principles of The Culture of Commerce[SM]. Remember that this is a leadership mindset that must become a team mindset quickly or the adoption rate has stalled. *(See graphic on next page)*

As the entire team mobilizes around the customer, they begin to think and behave at a higher level. Rather than acting as solo operators or teams working within silos or, worse yet, confined to their workflows, they begin to have a heightened awareness of how teams upstream or downstream of them are impacted by their workflows and how the customer experience is affected as a result. Remember, because every team has a customer, internal or external, we all influence the customer experience. As a first step, all teams should name their customer, whether it's a team or individuals in that team. By applying the five principles within The Culture of Commerce[SM], teams become problem-solvers and active participants in lubricating The Sales Engine[SM]. When the entire team is actively involved, The Culture of Commerce[SM] becomes a very powerful tool to END The Customer Prevention Culture[SM]. Let's explain how that happens.

The team begins to consider if the people, process and technology they interact with are in fact customer-centric (good) or company-centric (not good). They identify the culprit, determine if it's people, processes or technology, flag it and then quantify the impact to the customer by assigning a KPI, if one isn't already in place.

Similarly, the team will consider every customer touchpoint they impact and whether it

The Culture of Commerce℠ - The Remedy For The Customer Prevention Culture℠

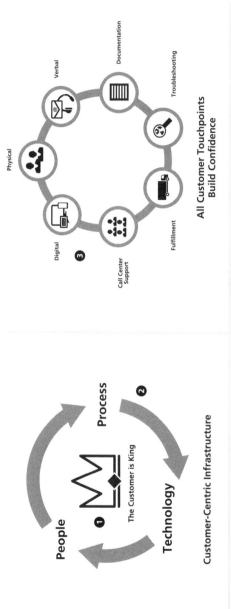

People

Process

Technology

① The Customer is King

② Customer-Centric Infrastructure

One Team - One Goal
Shared Organizational Outcomes
Through Maximum Alignment

④

Physical

Verbal

Documentation

Troubleshooting

Fulfillment

Call Center Support

Digital

③ **All Customer Touchpoints Build Confidence**

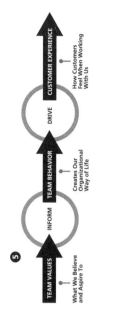

TEAM VALUES — What We Believe and Aspire To

INFORM

TEAM BEHAVIOR — Creates Our Organizational Way of Life

DRIVE

CUSTOMER EXPERIENCE — How Customers Feel When Working With Us

⑤ **Values Form Culture**

The Culture of Commerce℠ is Founded on the Following Principles:

1. The Customer is King!
2. Customer-Centric Infrastructure
3. All Customer Touchpoints Build or Break Confidence
4. One Team - One Goal
5. Values Form Culture

breaks or builds confidence. Specifically, teams whose workflows intersect collaborate on the customer touchpoints to determine if they're building or breaking confidence and review the company KPIs they believe their workflows impact. Team involvement gets more eyeballs on people, process and technology and provides multiple perspectives to move toward a customer-centric infrastructure. No longer are KPIs meaningless numbers that team members are held accountable to, but meaningful metrics that impact customer experience and create shared organizational outcomes. Most importantly, individuals and teams begin to understand why their workflow is critical to a customer outcome. Rather than feeling like they are making the proverbial mud pie, they associate their work with a higher purpose, which adds a sense of fulfillment to their work.

The team begins to take notice of their counterparts to assess if they are One Team – One Goal or have the tendency to work in a tribe or silo. My observation is that teams working in tribes or silos typically have a rogue leader or passive leadership and their team members simply fall in line. This is problematic. Adopters of The Culture of Commerce[SM] have a heightened sensitivity to tribes and silos and, as a result, identify outliers quickly. The job of the team is to shed light on outliers and come up with creative ways to maximize alignment. For certain, this would include more team training on The Culture of Commerce[SM] so team members understand the interdependency of the enterprise and the interconnectedness of workflows throughout the enterprise. Getting even more granular, rogue operators, passive leaders and team members working in tribes and silos will be reintroduced to team values, team behavior and how they affect the customer experience.

As we've learned, team values outline what we believe and aspire to, team behavior creates our organization's way of life and customer experience is how customers feel when working with us. Team Values inform Team Behavior, which drives Customer Experience. When employees bump up against friction within their own team, it becomes their job to call it out and pull in additional resources to redirect misaligned team members by teaching to the standard that is The Culture of Commerce[SM].

Team adoption of The Culture of Commerce[SM] ensures The Customer is King! But that cannot happen if the leadership mindset doesn't become a team mindset. The outcome of The Culture of Commerce[SM] is increased customer loyalty through vastly improved customer experience, greater team engagement and a framework that continuously sheds light on The Customer Prevention Culture[SM].

As the team begins to think, empathize and mobilize around the customer, the power of The Culture of Commerce[SM] takes shape and the customer experience improves in tangible ways. In The Customer Prevention Culture[SM], salespeople are the sales team. It's a lonely existence;

selling internally consumes most of their day and organizational resources are at odds with one another. In The Culture of Commerce^{SM}, salespeople notice the emergence of One Team – One Goal and what feels like The Sales Team as the entire organization adopts a customer-centric mindset. Salespeople are now unshackled to spend more time selling externally, and when they interface with their team members internally, they begin to see that customers are no longer considered a nuisance, but rather the reason for the company's existence.

RESOURCING THE SALES ENGINE WITH TIME, TALENT & CAPITAL
Ignite The Fuel

CHAPTER 9

"Fund it or fail it." —Unknown

Achieving sales goals is very much a numbers game, and there are no shortcuts. For me, this translates to answering the following questions:
- *How can I design my sales structure to maximize productivity?*
- *How can I resource The Sales Engine^{SM} to generate enough cycles to maximize the number of high-quality opportunities in my pipeline?*
- *How can I convert those high-quality opportunities into new customer relationships to achieve sales goals?*

Most sales teams have budget constraints while being challenged to produce results. Too often, B2B companies have a flawed sales model or their sales organization isn't resourced properly. Since we've addressed the sales model by introducing The Sales Engine^{SM}, let's now consider the different options for maximizing resources. Prior to resourcing The Sales Engine^{SM} with the optimal mix of time, talent and capital, determining the best sales channels to employ is the most effective first step for achieving sales results while managing the cost of sales.

(See graphics on next two pages)

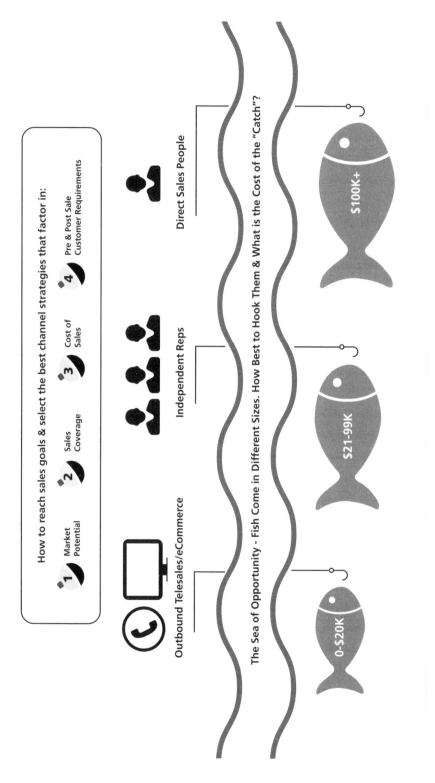

Building A Channel Strategy That Wins
Balancing Cost of Sales w/ Business Opportunities

How to reach sales goals & select the best channel strategies that factor in:

1. Market Potential
2. Sales Coverage
3. Cost of Sales
4. Pre & Post Sale Customer Requirements

Outbound Telesales/eCommerce

Independent Reps

Direct Sales People

The Sea of Opportunity - Fish Come in Different Sizes. How Best to Hook Them & What is the Cost of the "Catch"?

0-$20K

$21-99K

$100K+

Example Channel Strategy #1

THE**HALPIN**GROUP
©2019 The Halpin Group, LLC

Building A Channel Strategy That Wins *(Continued)*

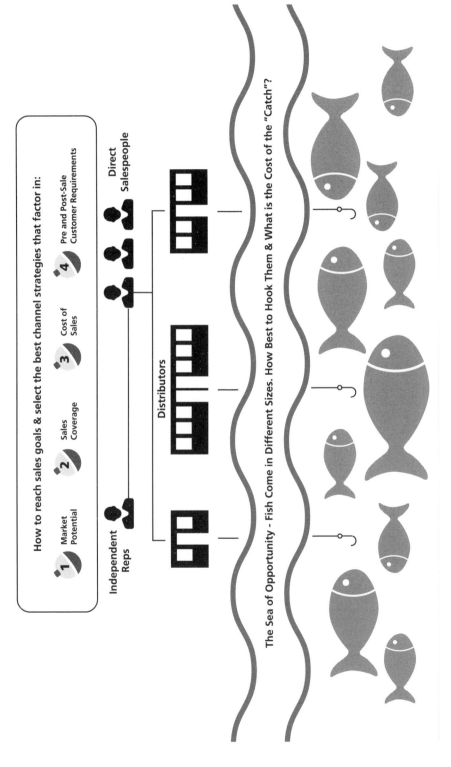

How to reach sales goals & select the best channel strategies that factor in:

1 Market Potential

2 Sales Coverage

3 Cost of Sales

4 Pre and Post-Sale Customer Requirements

Independent Reps

Distributors

Direct Salespeople

The Sea of Opportunity - Fish Come in Different Sizes. How Best to Hook Them & What is the Cost of the "Catch"?

Example Channel Strategy #2

THE**HALPIN**GROUP
©2019 The Halpin Group, LLC

Sales Channels

In most companies, there are good opportunities to develop multiple sales channels to grow sales with new and existing accounts. A sales channel *is a way of bringing products or services to market so they can be purchased by customers. A sales channel can be direct if it involves a business selling directly to its customers, or it can be indirect if an intermediary such as a dealer/distributor is involved in selling the product to customers.*[1]

The factors that weigh into determining the best sales channel strategy include:

• Market Potential

• Sales Coverage

• Cost of Sales

• Pre- and Post-Sale Customer Support

Additionally, a sales channel strategy should be married to a customer segmentation strategy. I recommend building a customer segmentation strategy based on customer groups with a range of account potential. In the graphic, you'll notice sample customer segments with account potential of less than $20,000, $21,000-99,000 and over $100,000. Even if a company sells into distinct verticals or supply chains, I still recommend breaking end users and customers into groups with a range of account potential. The way to think about customer segmentation is to consider how best to reach different segments based on their distinct needs and account potential while balancing the cost of sales. Consider how many customers make up the market and the company's ability to extend reach with the channel options available. Different sales channels might include:

• Direct Salespeople

• Independent Reps

• Outbound Telesales

• E-commerce

• Distributors, Resellers or Channel Partners

• Direct Mail

To start, it may make sense to determine which types of customers bring the highest value to the enterprise and the sales resources required to acquire and support them post-sale. This becomes your baseline, and then other sales channels and customer segments can be displayed based on their unique criteria.

(See graphic on next page)

The following factors need to be considered to arrive at the optimal multichannel sales strategy for your business.

---

[1] *http://www.businessdictionary.com/definition/sales-channel.html*

Pros and Cons of Different Sales Channels

Channel	Pros	Cons
Direct Sales	- 100% Mindshare - Ideal for Emerging Products	- High Fixed Cost - Low # of Customer Touches - Limited Sales Coverage
Independent Reps	- Variable Cost - Complementary Lines - Highly Scalable	- Partial Mindshare
Outbound Telesales	- Low Fixed Cost - High # of Customer Touches - Easy to Manage - 100% Mindshare	- Difficult to Manage Complex Sales
e-Commerce	- Customer Self-serve Option - Transacts 24/7/365 - Low Cost	- Limited Account Customization and Tech Support
Distribution	- Take Inventory Position - Ideal for Mature Products - One Stop Shop for End User - Strong Option for Fragmented Markets	- Brand Neutral - Partial Mindshare - Unique Value Can Get Lost

This table only intends to highlight the <u>major</u> points of distinction within different selling channels.

THE HALPIN GROUP
©2019 The Halpin Group, LLC

Standard Selling Channels in the B2B Marketplace

- **Market Potential** – What is the addressable opportunity in a given market? Addressable market potential is far more important than overall market size, as most businesses have a unique selling proposition that doesn't resonate with the entire market. The slice of the market that your business is targeting is your addressable market opportunity. For example, Starbucks isn't interested in the person who brews coffee at home or buys coffee at the local gas station. Those folks aren't likely part of Starbucks' addressable market. Coffee drinkers at large need to be segmented more narrowly for Starbucks and similar companies to arrive at their addressable market. The same goes for your business.

- **Sales Coverage** – Is your product line mature or emerging? Emerging products typically require heavy amounts of education and support to create market adoption. They also tend to have longer sales cycles. Mature products have achieved a high rate of adoption and the growth curve is near plateau. These considerations drive decision-marking in how best to support the product from a sales coverage perspective.

4 Stages of The Product Life Cycle

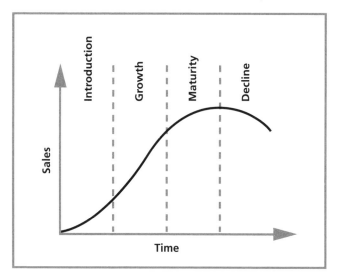

- Is your target market highly fragmented or highly concentrated? Fragmented markets tend to be supported through distribution to extend customer reach. Highly concentrated markets allow for different sales channel options such as direct salespeople, independent reps or outbound telesales.

- Which sales channels will provide the necessary number of customer touches and support the uniqueness of your sales cycle? Each sales cycle requires a different level of pre- and post-sale support.

Example: If 10,000 end users fit the profile of your target market, six direct salespeople will unlikely provide adequate coverage to achieve your true sales potential. However, selling to that number of end users through a distribution network or e-commerce may be a more realistic option. Of course, it's also helpful to understand if the 10,000 end users can be grouped into segments that reflect homogeneous buying characteristics. These are important considerations when determining which sales channels to employ to achieve growth targets.

Cost of Sales
- All sales channels have associated cost, but it's best to choose those that are scalable, sustainable and position your team to win.
- What is the total cost to your company to add one selling resource?
- Is a direct salesperson, independent rep, outbound telesales agent, e-commerce or distributor the best option to maximize the market opportunity?
- Can you segment the market and blend a channel strategy that makes sense for end-user types or market opportunities?
- Since free doesn't exist, settle on sales channels that can be replicated.

Pre- and Post-Sale Customer Requirements
Imagine the difference between selling magazine subscriptions and capital equipment. Or selling ERP software versus industrial supplies. Customer expectations and support before and after the sale dictate which channel strategies will be most effective. What works in shorter, simpler sales cycles won't necessarily transfer over to complex selling scenarios.

Many small and medium-sized businesses have one channel strategy for all verticals and all end-user types. This leads to a suboptimal situation, since different markets and end users respond to different hooks, methods and bait.

As you consider your sea of opportunity, begin to think differently about your channel strategy and align resources to drive sales success.

Time, Talent & Capital
For The Sales Engine[SM] to achieve scale, it must be resourced prudently with time, talent and capital. Your company's selling scenario, budget and sales goals will generally dictate the right balance of resources needed to make The Sales Engine[SM] perform. I began with sales channels because I've found B2B companies typically have opportunities to more intelligently allocate sales resources by thinking more broadly about how to touch more customers and grow their business by considering market potential, sales coverage, cost of sales and pre- and post-sale customer support.

When considering how to resource The Sales Engine[SM] with time, talent and capital, it's important to avoid what my friend Martin Doyle calls "magical thinking." Magical thinking is believing that a sales model or sales plan will deliver results without being resourced adequately. It's probably not a shocker that plans need to be resourced appropriately to yield results. Yet I've learned common wisdom is fairly uncommon. Let's further explore this idea together.

The Developing Story of Solid Springs NA

Michael Bell, general manager of Solid Springs, is one of my clients. Solid Springs is a manufacturer of mechanical compression springs and nitrogen gas springs, mainly used in metal stamping dies. They currently employ a multichannel sales strategy by selling through direct salespeople and distribution partners. A strong leader who is always looking for new ways to drive results, Michael recently invested in a comprehensive digital strategy including a new website, SEO services and paid search management with website-monitoring tools to track ROI. As a result, he is beginning to see consistent leads come through his company website.

However, he is also starting to understand the need to invest in an outbound telesales program so leads are jumped on quickly. Michael recently hired Sarah to validate an outbound telesales proof of concept to handle both the inbound website leads and call on his inactive account database. An inactive account is defined as a customer that placed an order 24 months ago but hasn't transacted since. Michael envisions Sarah implementing a multicall strategy to activate new accounts and reactivate inactive accounts. A reactivation occurs when the inactive account places a purchase order, Solid Springs becomes an active vendor and the customer orders regularly. Michael shared his philosophy with me a while back. He said, "One order doesn't make someone a customer. I consider someone a customer when they become a regular purchaser of product." I agree! For website lead follow-up, the goal is to activate the account and convert them into a regular purchasing customer through a nurturing or warming process.

The three-call sales strategy uses the three sales zones outlined earlier in The Defined Selling Process and The Sales Toolbox, and looks like this:

Call No. 1: During the first conversation, Sarah will NOT try to sell the prospect anything. This is Sales Zone No. 1, where the objective is Education & Exploration. She will simply introduce herself and Solid Springs with a focus on gathering information such as key decision-makers and learning as much as possible about the prospect's business. After the call, Sarah will send a follow-up email to the contact with one key asset from The Sales Toolbox and then enter a call summary into the CRM. The one key asset should be a slide, infographic or PDF that positions Solid Springs in the marketplace. The one key asset should tell a story and leave an impression resulting with the prospect thinking, "I get it — I understand Solid Springs and what they offer."

Ideally, the asset conveys a lot of different information such as:

- Market Position
- Market Offer
- Differentiators
- How You Add Value to Customer Relationships
- How Your Company Stacks Up Against Industry Peers

(For example, see the positioning graphic on Page 90)

This asset communicates information the prospect will find valuable in a single snapshot. If your company doesn't have an asset like this in The Sales Toolbox, I recommend creating one because of the meaningful conversations that follow.

Most salespeople fail to position their company within the broader market and instead jump to selling their widget, setting the stage for a transactional conversation. That's bad, by the way, because you've reduced the enterprise to yet another supplier of widgets or services. Savvy salespeople position their company in a thoughtful way by illustrating their knowledge of the marketplace and their position within it. Plotting your position on the intersection of price performance is the simplest method to follow, but not necessarily the only option. The inability to position your business in the context of the greater marketplace indicates a lack of strategy, which, in my mind, is lazy. What's typical and far less effective are assets such as a corporate capabilities brochure, line cards and videos highlighting the company's core business.

In her email, Sarah will include a subject line labeled, "Solid Springs Sales Rep," along with her contact information; she'll use a URL to deliver the asset so spam filters are less likely to block the email. The subject line is important in case the prospect cannot remember her name and needs to search his/her inbox to locate contact information. This would conclude a highly productive first call to an inactive account. If this is Call No. 1 following up on a website lead, Sarah would incorporate all of the above, but also address the immediate inquiry and then expand the conversation to better understand account potential, decision-makers and background on the prospect's business. In short, the goal is to have a high-quality first conversation that can be built upon in future calls. Sarah will have read Chapter 7 on Directed Conversations and Active Listening and, as a result, she will be dangerously equipped to engage in a high-impact call.

Call No. 2: During call No. 2, Sarah's objective is to quickly recap call No. 1 to reestablish a baseline with the customer. This is a way to refresh the customer's memory while verifying the information she gathered during call No. 1 remains accurate. She may inquire if the customer received her follow-up email and was able to review the one key asset (i.e., PDF, infographic or video). Now, Sarah can transition to asking impact questions that help to qualify the opportunity and determine account potential. Examples of impact questions include:

Positioning - Stand Out From The Crowd During The Sales Process

To Back Up Market Position:
- Clearly State Your Market Offer • Differentiators
- How That Creates Value For Customers

Addressable Market Opportunity

In One Snapshot, You're Able to:
- Convey Total Market Size • Addressable Market Opportunity • Market Position

Your Market Position

Competitor B

Competitor A

Competitor C

Performance

Demonstrate How You Stack Up!

Price

- Visual Tools Create More Meaningful Customer Conversations
- Inability to Position Indicates A Lack of Strategy

THE**HALPIN**GROUP
©2019 The Halpin Group, LLC

- How many employees do you have? How many of them work in your tool room?
- Who is your primary supplier of nitrogen gas springs/die springs? Are you pleased with them as a supplier? Could you give me a sense of the relationship, both what's working and areas for improvement?
- Can you explain your criteria for selecting the current supplier?
- It would help if I understood your annual spend on nitrogen gas springs or die springs. Would you be willing to share that information with me?
- Do you prefer to purchase direct from the manufacturer or through a local distributor?
- Have you ever experienced a product failure? If so, can you describe the failure mechanism?

I'm not suggesting Sarah ask all of these questions during Call No. 2, but the answers help her to understand potential fit and determine the next step.

You'll notice we're still not selling, but gathering information so we can build a game plan on how best to pursue the business, assuming there is a good fit (Sales Zone No. 2 – Fit Zone). We've all heard the phrase, "Know how to read the room." Selling by phone requires even more discerning skills because the seller doesn't have the ability to read body language. A skilled outbound telesales rep has the ability to "read the prospect" by listening for cues through pauses, tone of voice, questions and comments. A really strong seller knows how to ask questions, pause and listen. Additionally, outbound telesales reps know how to relax the prospect by talking slowly while also being succinct.

Assuming Call No. 2 leads Sarah to believe the prospect is a fit, she will then pull a different asset from The Sales Toolbox to advance the conversation to the next step. By the way, the objective of sharing an asset from The Sales Toolbox is not to attach it to an email, hit send and hope for the best. The goal is to use the asset to have a meaningful conversation with the prospect.

Now that Sarah has established a fit, she will direct the conversation to uncovering first opportunities to quote with the goal of securing the first purchase order. Sales Zone No. 3 is the part of the sales process focused on educating the customer on product offering, crossing over competitive part numbers, reviewing customer applications and directing customers into the appropriate solution. Equally as important, Sarah will teach the customer how to do business with Solid Springs on an ongoing basis by making introductions to key team members and setting accurate expectations for lead time, quote turnaround and order processing standards. Once Sarah successfully receives the first purchase order or two, she will transition the account to her customer service team and return to prospecting within the inactive account database and following up on website leads.

This story provides a few takeaways. One, Solid Springs provides a great example of appropriately funding a digital strategy and, two, avoids the trap of magical thinking by believing that investment alone will produce sales growth. Instead, they supported their investment in digital strategy by allocating a full-time resource assigned to website lead follow-up and inactive accounts. They've trained Sarah to use a multicall strategy, provided her with best practices for outbound callers and a Sales Toolbox of assets she can use to advance conversations. To truly measure the ROI of their digital strategy, Solid Springs now understands that nurturing leads is essential to maximizing lifetime customer value. They got there by using a holistic mindset and making a high level of commitment typical of those building The Sales Engine[SM].

(See graphic on next page)

Resourcing The Sales Engine[SM]

Time: The Sales Engine[SM] needs time and, more specifically, the cumulative time of individual salespeople working for the enterprise, directly or indirectly in the case of independent reps or distributors/resellers. If inadequately resourced with time, The Sales Engine[SM] will sputter because it won't have enough cycles. Each cycle is an individual sales sequence, sales opportunity or high-quality conversation. Sales teams must operate under the assumption that successfully landing new deals or new customer relationships will be proportional to the total number of cycles in process. As all sales professionals know, you win some, you lose some and others push. It's just the way the sales universe works. The number of cycles or high-quality conversations in process is a direct result of the cumulative time invested into The Sales Engine[SM].

Talent: The Sales Engine[SM] must be resourced with talent. I use the terms talent, people and teams interchangeably. If I were to identify one personality type for the highest impact on sales results and culture, I'd pursue humble leaders to build the dream team. I define a humble leader as someone who has a quiet confidence, strong work ethic and makes the environment better than they found it. Humble leaders naturally identify organizational gaps, propose solutions and have an action orientation. They make their teammates better because they openly share information, aren't threatened by constructive feedback and don't need to take credit. Humble leaders influence those they interact with because of their superior communication skills and contributions to team goals. Humble leaders are solid salespeople because of their ability to challenge customers and willingness to do the hard work required to be successful. Humble leaders know they are powerful, but don't need to boast because they aren't transactional people. They give freely of themselves because that's how they're hard-wired.

The talent component of time, talent and capital may be the most important resource of all because having the right people in place covers a multitude of sins. For example, if a company has suboptimal people, process and technology, adding the right talent will result in finding

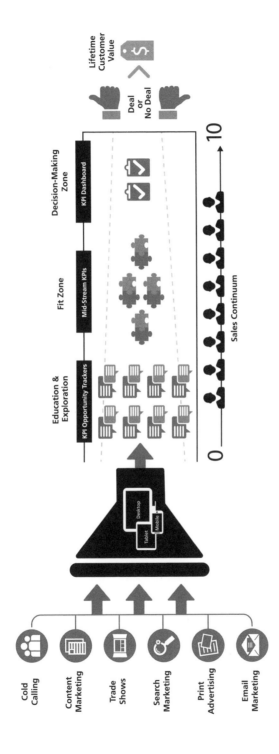

The Sales Engine
Growth Requires Generating Enough
Cycles & Advancing Them Through The Sales Process

New Customer Relationships Are Proportional
To The Total Number of Cycles In Process

THE**HALPIN**GROUP
©2019 The Halpin Group, LLC

solutions to mask the gaping holes in infrastructure (at least temporarily). Similarly, if The Sales Engine[SM] is resourced with the right talent, the Sales Toolbox and The Defined Selling Process will get better through their influence and contributions. The collaboration among The Sales Team will get better because humble leaders enjoy the transfer of knowledge and sharing of information to accomplish team goals. In short, securing the right talent multiplies the capacity of The Sales Engine[SM] and favorably impacts company culture at the same time. Talent is the force multiplier! People will always be an organization's greatest asset, and the ability to attract, hire and retain talent is a major differentiator between high-growth companies and those stuck riding the highs and lows of business cycles.

Capital: The Sales Engine[SM] requires financial capital to be properly resourced. Exactly how much capital can vary, but it's generally a function of many factors such as:
- Company Scale
- Growth Goals
- Selling Scenario Employed
- Sales Channel Strategy
- Competitive Landscape
- Addressable Market Opportunity

To simplify, it's about maximizing customer touches while managing the cost of sales.

As stated earlier, driving high-quality cycles through The Sales Engine[SM] is what creates new customer relationships and lifetime customer value (ROI). Capital is required to build and support an ongoing digital strategy, build high-value assets for The Sales Toolbox and support the cost structure of The Sales Team. More importantly, The Sales Engine[SM] is not a static framework. As resources are put in motion, the talent will provide data-driven feedback to improve the effectiveness and productivity of The Sales Engine[SM] over time and may require additional investment, all of which can be phased.

If lead generation is what fuels The Sales Engine[SM], then time, talent and capital trigger the ignition switch. By identifying the best sales channels to maximize customer touches and balance the cost of sales, companies are in the position to maximize the productivity of their resources.

Sales channels are particularly powerful when paired with a customer segmentation strategy. Customers truly have different needs and expectations, so attempting to provide coverage with a single sales channel is both costly and limiting. In my experience, one size fits all is a bad idea and I've yet to find a single sales team that wouldn't benefit from a multichannel sales strategy.

Once leadership determines the sales channel strategy that best supports their business goals, decisions can be made on how to resource The Sales Engine[SM] with time, talent and capital. It's understood that most companies are budget constrained in some form or fashion. However, The Sales Engine^{SM} can be implemented in phases by allowing specific components to be built over time. This enables adopters to validate proof of concepts, test the effectiveness of sales channels and then proceed with wider implementation.

Once a commitment is made for wider implementation, it's important to allocate resources for success. *Fund It or Fail It* is a concept worth considering for leaders responsible for allocating resources. I've learned that the level of resourcing often corresponds to the leadership's level of commitment. Stated another way, how projects are resourced reflects the attitude toward a project or initiative. As an example, I frequently see clients implement projects halfheartedly, almost as if they're planning to fail. Then, when the project isn't producing results, they respond, "See? I knew it wasn't going to work" — as if the project had a chance of success with the anemic level of resources it had to begin with. To ignite The Sales Engine^{SM}, total commitment and full funding are required, even if implemented in phases. Regardless of the implementation timeline, resource with the intent to succeed! To do otherwise will result in calling for roadside service.

WILL YOU JOIN ME ON THE MISSION?

CHAPTER **10**

"We see our customers as invited guests to a party, and we are the hosts. It's our job every day to make every important aspect of the customer experience a little bit better."
—*Jeff Bezos, Founder, CEO, Chairman and President, Amazon*

I hope you've found the content in this book to be helpful. The Sales Engine^{SM} is the roadmap to sales predictability and a business-agnostic framework applicable to transactional, solution-based and consultative selling scenarios. The Sales Engine^{SM} is for enterprises looking to close performance gaps among sales reps and reverse inconsistent sales results. Organizations struggling with this reality typically don't know what to do or how to do it. The Sales Engine^{SM} provides answers that enable sales leaders to focus on execution and coaching salespeople up or out of their organization.

Most companies are moderately successful and can point to something that works well, be it a strong product or service, pockets of committed team members, a compelling value proposition or other functional areas that contribute to their sales success. But moderately successful companies have an engine that's not quite firing on all cylinders. The Sales Engine^{SM} is a cohesive sales and marketing strategy that is simple, effective and irrefutable. Many thought leaders over-complicate sales. The Sales Engine^{SM} is a simplified sales process that both salespeople and their counterparts can easily understand.

When implemented properly, The Sales Engine[SM] provides adopters with an abundance of high-quality opportunities flowing through their pipeline and puts them in position to close a fair share of sales. The return on investment (ROI) of The Sales Engine[SM] is lifetime customer value which, in most cases, indicates companies will enjoy recurring customer relationships. However, The Sales Engine[SM] is limited without a winning culture to support it. After all, the atmosphere, attitudes and behavior in which business is conducted throughout the customer life cycle is how disciples are created.

My why for writing this book is to help B2B companies address the plague of The Customer Prevention Culture[SM] so widespread in business today. I'm passionate about this topic because, as the owner/operator of an independent sales agency, I've battled The Customer Prevention Culture[SM] with many of the companies I've represented. I've found team mindsets, people, process and technology to be at odds with frictionless commerce, causing sales teams to intervene and shield customers from the dysfunction. It's absurd to think any person, team or organization would intentionally set out to build The Customer Prevention Culture[SM], and yet experience validates these challenges are the rule rather than the exception.

In the rare instances I encounter The Culture of Commerce[SM] mindset, I usually find a strong leader or charismatic entrepreneur with high standards or, in the case of a larger company, leadership that's completely sold out to creating the best customer experience possible. Consider the number of times you've personally experienced incredible customer service, or the number of times you've been wowed by customer care. Maybe five times in 100? Imagine the negative impact to commerce when The Customer Prevention Culture[SM] is allowed to persist in a business. It's costly and unacceptable.

So how do we end it? The answer lies in building awareness that The Customer Prevention Culture[SM] exists, calling it out and offering The Culture of Commerce[SM] as a solution. My goal is for The Customer Prevention Culture[SM] and The Culture of Commerce[SM] to become part of our everyday language so when we experience one or the other, we can name it and either address it or build on it. Too often we're aware elements of The Customer Prevention Culture[SM] exist in our business, but blow it off because we don't want to confront it. There may be people to take on, internal selling to perform or systemic issues to challenge. It may require taking on highly defensive caretakers of people, process and technology within our organizations, and it seems daunting.

My question is: *What's the alternative?* Accept mediocrity? Being okay with offering a substandard customer experience? In the end, isn't this exactly the kind of action required of leaders? To challenge institutional thinking and move our company toward a better future state? I don't see a choice but to confront it, but to do so, we must offer the solution. When considering the amount of disruption facing B2B companies globally, leaders must acknowledge the need to either adapt or die. I wonder why we accept self-inflicted wounds like The Customer Prevention Culture^{SM} and allow it to set up camp in our companies. It makes no sense, and the only plausible reason for it is passive leadership.

I hope I've challenged your thinking and that you're sold on The Culture of Commerce^{SM}. More importantly, I hope you decide to join me on the mission. Your participation could help eliminate The Customer Prevention Culture^{SM} forever.

As a leadership mindset, The Culture of Commerce^{SM} is essential for companies to grow and thrive. But I need your help. I need you to adopt this leadership mindset and introduce it to your colleagues and peers. Without your help, The Culture of Commerce^{SM} won't have the reach required and businesses won't be transformed to their full potential.

Think of the possibilities. If we remedy the Customer Prevention Culture^{SM}, we can return to doing business with the U.S. Postal Service — not because of Stockholm Syndrome, but because it has won our confidence. We can call the rental company and trust the truck is being booked in the U.S., rather than in another country. We can circle back with the inside sales representative who's perpetually rude and request a quick turnaround for the new account, knowing we're now on the same page. We can confidently address customer service issues with a client knowing we're aligned with a common vision. Life will be far better! Adopting The Culture of Commerce^{SM} doesn't make all elements of The Customer Prevention Culture^{SM} go away immediately, but it does align and direct resources toward a shared standard and vision. As leaders, we have an obligation to wisely steward the resources entrusted to us. The Culture of Commerce^{SM} points us to a higher standard to build culture, drive sales and create disciples.

Parting Gift

You may be thinking, "The Customer Prevention Culture^{SM} exists in my organization and I'd like to bring it to the attention of my team, or I'd like to introduce The Culture of Commerce^{SM} to my co-workers. But I don't know where to start."

These are reasonable thoughts. To gauge the current state of your company culture, we've created The Culture of Commerce^{SM} Assessment Tool. It allows individuals to sign in, assess their organization across several functional areas and receive an overall score. By providing their name and email, users will receive a PDF summary document explaining their results and recommendations. Companies could have several team members and customers run through the assessment and then manually tabulate the scores. For companies that require customization of the assessment and a summary or dashboard, submit an inquiry through my website and we'll schedule a conversation.

Interested parties can access The Culture of Commerce^{SM} Assessment Tool at *thehalpingroup. net/culture-of-commerce-assessment or by scanning the QR code on the opposite page.*

A snapshot of The Culture of Commerce^{SM} Assessment Tool is provided here to give readers a sense of how it works.

The intent of The Culture of Commerce^{SM} Assessment Tool is for leaders to consider common customer touchpoints, the interdependencies of each functional area on customer experience and the workflows causing friction in their organization.

One final plea to those of you who wield influence in your company: Please don't settle for mediocrity by falling into the trap of passive leadership. Your team, customers and company deserve better!

Scan me

тнеHALPINGROUP
The Culture of Commerce℠ Index

1. Front Office/Customer Facing

	Best Practices	Emerging	Average	Unsatisfactory	At Risk
Sales	○	○	○	○	○
Marketing	○	○	○	○	○
Customer Service	○	○	○	○	○
Technical Support	○	○	○	○	○
Aftermarket Service	○	○	○	○	○
Quality	○	○	○	○	○

2. Back Office/Non-Customer Facing

	Best Practices	Emerging	Average	Unsatisfactory	At Risk
Fulfillment/Operations	○	○	○	○	○
Engineering	○	○	○	○	○
Shipping/Receiving	○	○	○	○	○
Accounts Receivable	○	○	○	○	○
Accounts Payable	○	○	○	○	○
Information Technology	○	○	○	○	○
Human Resources	○	○	○	○	○
Supply Chain	○	○	○	○	○

Complete

WHAT PEOPLE ARE SAYING ...

"Tom Halpin articulates fresh perspectives and clear insights on the entire sales process — highlighting opportunities that exist at most companies. Additionally, he provides specific tools to reduce pain-points which ultimately will garner more sales. Tom's personal communication style, succinct examples and clear explanations precisely describe the situations. Likewise, his problem-solving frameworks bring a robust structure to the solutions."

—**Bill Wolins,** VP Sales and Marketing, UTILCO

"Too often companies lose focus on the lifeblood of their existence — a positive customer experience. The Customer Prevention Culture *reminds all of us to never accept customer apathy within our organization."*

—**Kevin D. Guy,** Managing Partner/Cofounder, Wellington Private Capital

"We have been working with Tom for over five years now and he's always given us real-time sales and marketing advice that we can use to improve our business. After reading The Customer Prevention Culture, *we are rethinking and examining the sales and service experience we deliver."*

—**Sal Garbarino,** VP Sales & Marketing, RTS Cutting Tools

"Tom does a masterful job of framing The Customer Prevention Culture, *allowing the reader to see and recognize how these challenges creep into an organization, and then offers straightforward insight on how to respond. This is a must read for any business owner or sales professional looking to build a sales and service culture that continually seeks to maximize their opportunities."*

—**Karl Ganshirt,** President, Global Tooling Solutions LLC

"I've known Tom Halpin for approximately 20-plus years and was fortunate to work with him in prior employment. Tom's intellectual, consultative selling style developed strong customer relationships while delivering significant sales results. I look forward to sharing The Customer Prevention Culture *with the leaders in our organization who are also interested in maintaining a customer experience void of friction and frustration."*

—David Lange, North American Sales Manager, Incoe Corporation

"Tom Halpin presents an incredibly accurate description of the challenges we as managers face both internally and externally. Often times the challenges of managing our business, we create ourselves by focusing on the wrong things. The Customer Prevention Culture *is not just the best description I have read on addressing the issues of turning prospects into long-term customers, but also the antidote to improving the sustainable health of my business."*

—John E. Hill, President/CEO, Midwest Mold Services Inc.

"Tom Halpin taps his industrial B2B sales experience to offer insights and solutions to maximize customer loyalty."

—Tom Bell, Executive Director-Specialty Steel, Hitachi Metals America LTD.

ABOUT THE AUTHOR

Tom Halpin is a sales and marketing leader, a student of business and someone who has practiced his trade at a high level for more than 20 years. By adapting to successfully sell different products and services at various points in his career, his teams have produced more than $150 million in sales in a wide range of deal sizes. For the last 15 years, he has owned and operated an independent sales agency, having represented 40 different companies and sold to hundreds of customers in a variety of verticals. His experience is unique in that he has sold steel, software, mature products, engineered products, services and consulting. This

Tom Halpin

background has produced an expertise in transactional, consultative and solution-based sales scenarios. He has sold directly to end users, through channel partners and to different buyer personas, ranging from business owners to engineers and purchasers to other influencers. In the area of simple and complex B2B selling scenarios, few bring as much to the conversation.

Through this experience, Tom has developed a passion for customer experience, sales predictability and the hard work required of companies striving to stand out in the marketplace.

Tom's ability to challenge institutional thinking helps clients flush out mindsets and decision-making patterns that are incongruent with their business goals. For him, nothing beats creating, testing and implementing strategy to deliver meaningful business outcomes for clients.